MW00616771

If You Can't Beat 'em, Join 'em

If You Can't Beat 'em, Join 'em

Jim Mosteller

Amalia Publishing

If You Can't Beat 'em, Join 'em
Copyright © 2007 by Jim Mosteller
Published by Amalia Publishing

All rights reserved. No part of this book may be reproduced (except for inclusion in reviews), disseminated or utilized in any form or by any means, electronic or mechanical, including photocopying, recording, or in any information storage and retrieval system, or the Internet/World Wide Web without written permission from the author or publisher.

This publication is designed to provide accurate and authoritative information in regard to the subject matter covered. It is sold with the understanding that neither the author nor the publisher is engaged in rendering financial, accounting, legal, or other professional services by publishing this book. If financial advice or other expert assistance is needed, the service of a competent professional should be sought. The author and publisher specifically disclaim any liability, loss or risk resulting from the use or application of the information contained in this book.

For further information, please contact:
Office: 800-569-0413
jim@libertyassetmgt.com

BOOK DESIGN BY
ARBOR BOOKS, INC.
19 SPEAR ROAD, SUITE 301
RAMSEY, NJ 07446

JACKET DESIGN AND PHOTOS BY
NATHAN HADWEN, BEST PHOTOGRAPHY

PRINTED IN UNITED STATES

TITLE AUTHOR 1. TITLE 2. AUTHOR
3.PERSONAL FINANCE & INVESTING/ESTATE PLANNING

LIBRARY OF CONGRESS CONTROL NUMBER: 2006909784
ISBN 10: 0-9791137-0-9
ISBN 13: 978-0-9791137-0-3

For Jenny, Kate, Claire and Allison

If You Can't Beat 'em, Join 'em

CONTENTS

INTRODUCTION

Retiring Free of Financial Worries

Most of us, during retirement, would like to be able to lock the barn door on our assets with the expectation of finding them still there, in good shape, on future periodic visits. That may be your dream, and it is of course unrealistic, but in this book I offer you the next best thing—how to go on with your life secure in the knowledge that your investment assets are being managed not by hunches and vested interests but by rock-solid academic analysis.

As a lawyer and licensed financial advisor, I am very careful about the assurances I give. There's no magic or mystery about the investment approach offered in this book. It is my objective that all clients receive financial advice based on proven academic research.

To be a successful investor, you need a disciplined and consistent strategy. The objective is to enhance clients' wealth by controlling risk, with the goal of realizing growth through a diversified and cost-efficient investment portfolio. Risk is best managed through portfolio diversification.

1

The structure of each individual's portfolio should be designed to match his or her personal aims and circumstances. Typically, each portfolio consists of investments representing various asset classes, utilized as needed to create a diversified investment account. Generally speaking, when creating such a portfolio by using the services of a registered investment advisor (more on this in Chapter 9), a fee is charged that is not dependent on the investment vehicle or trading activity. In contrast, when creating a portfolio by using the services of a broker, a commission is typically charged for each transaction.

The path you take is a matter of personal preference, and a thorough understanding of what you are paying for when searching for a financial advisor is important. That said, I believe the services provided by a registered investment advisor provide a client with unbiased advice that is in the client's best interest. It is for this reason that we chose to create Liberty Asset Management and bring this level of service to our clients.

Fundamental Concepts

At our firm, we base our financial advice on some fundamental concepts of markets today. We didn't originate these concepts and there's nothing strange or radical about them. In fact, many advisors to big companies and very wealthy people base their financial advice on them.

Most individual investors, however, even when they are aware of these concepts, find it difficult to make practical use of them. I am both pleased and proud that I have been able to change that and make these same strategies available to the average retiree.

Here are the five fundamental concepts of our investment philosophy:

- **Markets are efficient.** Market prices, at any given time, reflect the expectations of investors. In other words, an efficient market means that what you pay for a stock, bond, or mutual fund is what you should be paying.

2

- **Your portfolio structure is important.** Asset allocation principally determines results in a broadly diversified portfolio. You want to take advantage of the risks that offer a reward and avoid those that do not.

- **Manage risk through diversification.** Broad diversification is key to managing a portfolio and reducing uncertainty.

- **Control investment costs.** Transaction costs and investment fees can consume profits. Avoiding unnecessary turnover and using funds with institutional-type pricing can slow this cash drain.

- **Time is your friend.** The longer the time horizon, the less price volatility affects a diversified portfolio.

Most investors have no trouble accepting these concepts. It's only when it comes to making practical use of them, as I said, that they run into difficulties.

Take the first concept, about markets being efficient, as an example. If you decide to buy a stock selling at 20, you obviously believe that its price will increase. But if you accept the concept that the stock market is efficient, you have to consider that other investors may disagree that the price will rise, and that they are willing to get rid of the stock at 20.

What do you know that they don't? Indeed, you may know something. Even if you don't and are relying on a hunch, you may prove to be right. Hunches can also produce big winnings at a casino or racetrack, but they don't add up to a reliable investment philosophy.

Our approach to investment decisions centers on how particular stocks behave in relation to other stocks in an investor's portfolio, rather than just how they behave in relation to the market as a whole. This approach, known as *Modern Portfolio Theory,* won a Nobel Prize for its originators at the University of Chicago. But it's not just an academic exercise. Using it can help you eliminate the need to make the kind of investment decisions that are really only hopeful guesses.

Diversification and Asset Allocation

Avoiding loss is a tried and true way to ensure profit. Activity in any market, however, entails the risk of loss. As an investor, you can't avoid risk entirely, but you can protect yourself in various ways.

Protection of assets is a major feature of this book. I agree with whoever first said that keeping what you already own can be the hardest work of all. Diversifying your investments over a range of asset classes helps you to manage risk through not putting too many eggs into any one basket. It's as simple as that.

Some investors imagine that they are diversifying their portfolios when they buy shares in Kellogg as well as Kraft. But, of course, they are still investing in food companies. If they had bought Merck instead of Kellogg, that would have at least been diversification into a drug company.

However, both companies can be classified as "large cap" stocks and therefore their purchase does not result in complete diversification when delving into the finer points of asset allocation.

But, investors tend to stay with what they know. When presented with the challenge of something new, it's easy to turn away and seek reassurance from the familiar. They may not even be conscious they are doing it. However, while owning shares in six different food companies may be better than owning shares in one, it does not amount to portfolio diversification.

Asset allocation, the most effective way to achieve portfolio diversification, goes way beyond tinkering with different kinds of stocks. The process divides your investment portfolio into a number of major asset classes, such as domestic large equity growth and value funds, domestic small equity growth and value funds, real estate funds, international funds, bond funds, and so on.

The number and relative sizes of these classes are tailored to the individual investor's aims and circumstances.

Studies have shown that asset allocation is the single most important factor in determining results from investing.

We work with clients to determine what allocation of assets can best help them achieve their financial goals. We monitor portfolios to ensure that investment plans stay on course to meet investor needs. Overall, we focus our efforts on developing portfolios that build wealth over the years, regardless of market conditions.

Were You My Client...
In this book, I try to treat you like I would one of my clients at Liberty Asset Management. Of course, I'm limited by the fact that I don't know you personally and don't know your financial circumstances.

But I won't let these limitations prevent me from communicating to you the essential elements of a disciplined investment strategy. I'll be happy if I succeed, through these chapters, in getting you to look at the following topics in a fresh way:

- Building a portfolio compatible with your investment aims and risk tolerance.

- Minimizing the transaction costs and investment fees that eat up so much profit.

- Monitoring and rebalancing your portfolio as your investment goals change and markets shift and evolve.

While a disciplined investment strategy is the main thrust of this book, other chapters cover different financial aspects of retiring Many books are already available on retirement planning and so forth, and I won't cover that familiar ground.

Much of what I have to say on various subjects relates to people who possess modest to substantial assets and are now retired or are on the verge of retiring. My message is that your retirement can be much more secure and stress free with the advice of an experienced and caring professional.

Investing and Retirement

Many people wonder how they will fill their days during retirement. In the first chapter, we discuss how beginning your retirement may be one of the most intensely active and decisive periods of your life. Far from fading gently into the sunset, you are presented with many issues to resolve. How you resolve them determines to a great extent the quality of your retirement.

The chapters in Part I cover what you need to know. The second chapter takes a positive financial viewpoint, indicating how your money can increase over time and how assets grow in value.

We compare active and passive investing in Chapter 3. Active investors try to pick individual stocks that turn out to be big winners, while passive investors select whole market segments of stocks, usually in the form of an index. We discuss how stock prices in an efficient market reflect the opinions of investors. Thus, when you buy a stock with the expectation of an increase in its price, you are really saying you know something that the rest of us do not.

Additionally, we look at the unpredictability of markets and how, in order to have a successful investment experience, you need to invest passively, give your investments time, and get professional advice.

High returns on investments usually involve high risk. During retirement, investors generally accept the fact that they no longer have time to recover from big losses. Therefore, they are usually willing to trade high levels of profit and risk for more acceptable lower levels.

However, there are other ways to lower risk. In Chapter 4, we examine the risk-lowering strategy of diversification. We see why asset allocation is oftentimes considered the most efficient way to achieve diversification of your portfolio in an efficient market.

Chapters 6 through 8 review the assets you probably hold and the options these assets offer you during retirement.

In Chapter 9, we look at how an experienced, competent professional advisor can more or less make your retirement financially worry free.

Benefits of Estate Planning

Most of us want to provide for those we leave behind. We may have strong wishes about our bequests. In Chapter 10, we list four options you have in estate planning—two of which involve doing little or nothing. This chapter will help you make up your mind about what really matters to you.

We talk about whether you should make a will in Chapter 11, and what should and should not be in it. Probate, an often lengthy and expensive legal process, is a major drawback of having a will. We consider the circumstances in which probate can be avoided and when, in my opinion, it is not worth avoiding.

There are ways to pass on assets to beneficiaries outside a will that avoid the delay of probate. We briefly review these ways in Chapter 12. Trusts are an important way to pass on assets to your heirs without delay or interference, and we look at how a trust works in this chapter.

In Chapter 13, we describe how to set up a living trust—the kind you can contribute to during your lifetime. You see what is involved in starting a "dynasty trust" in Chapter 14—the kind of trust that can pass on assets from generation to generation without estate taxes or generation-skipping taxes.

Your children and grandchildren may feel uncomfortable about discussing their inheritance with you. You may also have some concerns about their attitudes toward financial matters. Chapter 15 has some insights and good advice on these issues.

What This Book Can Do for You

When it comes time to retire, we often have to deal with things we have been putting off for years. Also, things we have never really considered before can suddenly assume importance. Some of these issues, if not resolved properly, can have a lasting effect on your lifestyle.

Instead of flailing about, you can use this book to take a safe and rewarding approach to investing for retirement and planning your estate. You have worked hard for your assets, and now you need to protect them. They are your guarantee of a comfortable retirement after a long career. This book shows you how to treat them with the care they deserve, so that they in turn can contribute to the quality of your life.

In retirement, we need to be more concerned with holding on to what we have rather than making risky ventures in search of high returns. This book explains why investment strategies based on academic analysis provide much more security for retirees than stock picking through guesswork and hunches.

The academic work behind this methodology can generally be called *Modern Portfolio Theory.* "Ranching" is an analogy I use in getting people to realize that today, there are better ways to invest. At the present time, you can still go out riding the range with cowboys—but everyone knows that usually it's just for fun and for the nostalgia of days gone by. Serious ranchers, though, use high-tech livestock management systems that outperform anything a cowboy ever dreamed of achieving.

Similarly, while stock picking can be fun as a pastime, from an investment point of view it is an old cowboy way of managing money. *Modern Portfolio Theory*, making use of today's technology, is a far more rewarding way of "ranching" investment returns.

Safer, more secure ways of retirement investing are available to everyone. This book explains what they are and how to use them. Through trusts and estate planning, you can add more retirement safeguards and make provisions for those close to you. After you read this book, you can make life-enhancing decisions with new confidence and tranquility.

PART I

INVESTING FOR YOUR QUALITY OF LIFE

CHAPTER ONE

Retirement and Decisive Action

Upon retirement, you should be able to focus on enjoying life and not have to worry from day to day about investment decisions, what will happen to your estate, and whether you have done everything you needed to do.

To get the best out of life, you need to free yourself from these concerns. I try to show you how to do that in this book. There are ways to invest in a disciplined and sensible manner so that you can go out and enjoy life. There are also reliable ways to pass your assets on to your loved ones, children, grandchildren, or a charity.

For decades, the very wealthy have utilized investment managers, life insurance specialists, estate planning attorneys, and tax professionals. You don't need to have $20 million to benefit from this kind of advice. In this book, I bring this service to you.

Why do you need advice? Why not do it yourself? You may be one of the top people in your line of work, the best at what you do, but your skills in that field won't necessarily translate into an ability to manage your assets. Some successful people find this hard to concede. If they excel at one thing, why should they not be good at another?

Often, it's because they haven't put the same time and effort into it. They see people they consider to be less investment-savvy than they are do well in the markets, so they think that it can't be all that difficult. What many find, though, is that while it's easy to buy, it's just as easy to get burned. In fact, there's a Wall Street joke about it being too late for traders to get out of a stock when doctors start buying it.

People like to imagine that their exits from working life will be gentle fadeouts, but oftentimes they are just the opposite. Even when many of the necessary decisions have been made in advance, there are frequently many things to be done after retirement has begun.

Some people leave almost everything until nearly the last moment. Then, in a frantic period, they have to tie up all the loose ends of their business careers while making instant decisions about daily living and financial management.

During the time when you are winding down your work activities or selling your business in preparation for retirement, you are faced with multiple other decisions that will have a lasting impact on how you live. Doing everything at one time in a short, intense period is the way a lot of people like to handle this challenge. The problem: you may have to live with these rushed decisions over a long time frame.

I always tell people to keep things as simple as possible going into retirement. Some decisions depend on individual taste—you must make the choice yourself. In such circumstances, what you need to do is allow yourself time in which to make a decision that is not unnecessarily (and possibly negatively) influenced by other factors.

However, asset management and similar decisions often require a professional level of knowledge. At this point in your life, it is usually not a good time to start reading books on "get rich quick" Wall Street strategies or how to make a million bucks in real estate. Such projects almost always entail high risk. Your best strategy is to hold on to what you've got and not lose it by making rash or impulsive decisions.

If you're trying to make your mind up whether to trade down in house size and buy a resort condo; move full-time to Colorado; stay put and start a new small business; leave money in trust for the education of your grandchildren; take a world cruise; or volunteer for a nonprofit cause, this may not be the best time to make investment and estate planning decisions that will have an effect on the rest of your life and beyond.

Having a skilled and experienced professional to advise you on such financial matters, someone you can totally trust, benefits you emotionally as well as monetarily. Medical researchers have shown that reducing your stress level over money concerns can boost good health, promote healing, and contribute to longevity.

I'm not making health claims about my financial advice! I simply want you to understand the potential value of planning for the future, so that you can enjoy living today.

We will look further at finding a trustworthy, licensed financial advisor in Chapter 9.

Some Popular Delusions
When you ask people what they plan to do when they retire, many answer, "Play golf." That may be about as far as their thinking has gone, although they know that a leisurely retirement centered on golf probably requires financial planning and management.

However, practically speaking, it requires much less effort to daydream than to plan. Some of those dreamers never make it to the fairway because of their lack of financial management. They belong to the biggest group with delusions or illusions about retirement: they believe that even if they do nothing, things will work out.

Certainly, things will work out, but not necessarily to their advantage. Most of us realize that doing nothing actually amounts to doing something—it's a management decision.

Some people continually put off or refuse to think about decisions they know they will have to make someday. We all know otherwise reliable and responsible people like this; they simply do not want to talk or think about retirement. Some claim they will *never* retire—that they will work until they drop. And they may have to if they don't make some effort to manage their finances.

Then, there are those who say they are going to spend all of their money. They may be forced to do so without proper planning.

Others with pensions and retirement plans neglect reviewing them. They vaguely assume that their living costs will be less after retirement, although the opposite can be the case. They think they will be all right when they add Social Security to the income they know they will have.

The sad truth is that a pension and Social Security often amount to only one-third of a retired person's financial needs. For someone with a wise investment strategy, income and appreciation from assets can make up the shortfall and help improve that person's quality of life.

Some Questions
When? How well? And where? These are the questions most of us need answers to upon retirement. These questions clearly have a bearing on planning for the future.

When Are You Retiring?
Retirement at 65, with a pension adequate for a carefree life of leisure, may have been a reality in the past but is now something that few of us can depend on. We know what inflation can do in just a few years to a fixed pension, and fewer and fewer people remain in pensioned employment to the age of 65. Some find themselves

in forced retirement while still in their 40s. Having a second career today is often a matter of necessity rather than choice.

After leaving the full-time work force, you may be able to continue in your line of work as an independent consultant or contractor for some years, but almost inevitably, you begin to lose touch with the latest developments and start to notice how your contacts in companies are increasingly becoming independent consultants or contractors themselves.

Even then, it can be hard to let go. In fact, there may be no reason to, if you enjoy the work and derive some income from it. However, you need to factor in a declining income to create a sound plan for the future.

How Well Will You Live?

Your post-retirement lifestyle expectations may or may not be realistic. Without giving the matter much thought, some of us expect to live quite lavishly on a reduced income and modest assets.

You'll have more free time on your hands. If your needs are few and your tastes inexpensive, you'll have a great time. But if you required more than contemplation, birdsong, and spring water for entertainment during your working years, you are likely to continue doing so in retirement.

Where Are You Retiring?

Are you staying where you are, moving elsewhere for part of the year, or starting a new life in a different place?

Moving for part of the year may require the upkeep of two homes. The cost of living in a new place can be hard to estimate. Expensive locations are often even more expensive than they are reputed to be and so-called "reasonably priced" places may turn out to be anything but the bargain you thought you were getting. Additionally, don't forget the unanticipated costs frequently encountered when moving homes.

Determining Your Net Worth

In order to make realistic arrangements for retirement, you need to know your net worth. The key word here is *realistic*, because the size of your net worth is likely to be a controlling factor in what is achievable in crafting your retirement plans.

Your net worth is simply the sum of your assets less the sum of your liabilities. If your spouse has assets or liabilities in his or her name, it may be best to make up three separate net worth statements: what's in your name, what's in your spouse's name, and what's jointly held.

It's easy to forget assets, especially those you have held for a long time. As a reminder, here's a list of assets that probably includes most of what you hold:

- **Cash**
- **Checking accounts**
- **Savings accounts**
- **Money market accounts**
- **Certificates of deposit**
- **IRA account**
- **Keogh account**
- **Employee savings plan**
- **Life insurance**
- **Annuities**
- **Stocks**
- **Bonds**
- **Treasury bonds, bills, and notes**
- **Mutual funds**
- **Home value**
- **Second home and real estate investments**
- **Cars, boats, etc.**
- **Jewelry and other valuables (professionally appraised)**
- **Collectibles (professionally appraised)**
- **Receivables likely to be paid**
- **Deferred income**

The list of liabilities is much shorter and you are less likely to need reminding about them:

- **Mortgages**
- **Taxes unpaid**
- **Credit card balances**
- **Loans (car, home equity, personal, etc.)**
- **Major bills unpaid (home repair, major medical bills, brokerage margins, etc.)**

Why You Need to Invest

I hope I have convinced you by now that the process of retiring is usually nothing like sailing into a peaceful sunset. You may already know this and could even add a few trials of your own to my list. If so, you will agree with me that a person about to retire, in the act of retiring, or just having retired, needs to take decisive action.

Some of the decisions that need to be made and actions that need to be taken concern daily living. Some concern the management of assets. And still others concern your wishes regarding the handling of your estate when you pass away. In any event, the first step in this process is to determine your overall objective— that is, maintaining a comfortable retirement income while providing for moderate growth in order to stay ahead of inflation.

You then must find a trusted professional to help you implement a sound investment strategy and estate plan that will serve you today and in the future. You want to find someone to "mind the store," so to speak, so that you can go out and enjoy life. Providing you with sound ideas relating to investment management and estate planning are the two main concerns of this book.

We will start out with assets, markets, and investments. When you mention the word investments, people tend to assume that you are talking about stocks and the stock markets. An important part of my advice to you is that you need to diversify by investing beyond the stock markets. But it makes sense to start out on familiar ground.

The opening years of this new century saw devastating stock market losses. According to one survey, from spring 2000 to December 2002, more than 97 percent of Americans with $100,000 to $1 million invested lost money, and more than 1 in 3 lost more than half their money.

Many of these people were sophisticated investors with years of stock market experience and they were advised by the most highly regarded "experts" in the industry. Their losses—in many cases, the total destruction of their wealth—were caused by the popping of a high tech stocks bubble. In hindsight, when the excitement of the time has subsided, explanation becomes easy.

There is much to be learned from the misfortune of others. Preventing it from happening to ourselves is a strong motivation to learn. But why invest at all if this sort of thing can happen to you? Because…if you want to live well in retirement, you most likely have no alternative to investing.

To run away from the stock markets is the wrong response. It is our philosophy that you must maintain a *disciplined* and sound strategy based on your desired level of risk and return to have a truly successful investment experience.

Investment Income and Inflation
I admire the candor of one financial writer in admitting the mistakes she made in her own investment strategy.

In spite of regarding herself as a savvy investor and having written professionally for 15 years on money, investing, and personal finance, she found that she had been putting her money in the wrong places. She stashed her dollars away on a regular basis in conservative accounts such as bonds, money market funds, and Treasury bills—and then forgot about them.

Even when interest rates are high, this is not necessarily the wisest thing to do. When rates dipped to the low single digits, she was earning an annual return of about four percent—not much above the inflation rate. In other words, the value (or purchasing power) of her money was almost standing in place, rather than steadily increasing over time.

If you sold all your assets and put all your money into a risk-free, no-interest account, your money would lose about three percent of its value each year at the present time because of inflation. You would become gradually poorer.

If the inflation rate jumped to 10 percent, your cash would lose one-tenth of its purchasing power each year. Investing is your best protection against inflation, because the value of stocks is likely to rise at a higher rate than inflation.

A friend was surprised to learn that his long-retired prosperous father's pension was tiny by today's standards. Had it not been for the investments he made, his father told him, the son would have grown up in near poverty instead of the prosperity he took for granted.

Investment Aims

What do I mean by investment aims? Consider two people who actively invest in the stock market. Tom enjoys the excitement of trying to pick winners and raking in cash when he is right. That's basically why he "plays" the market.

Harry, on the other hand, has long-term investment goals. He knows where he is today, knows where he wants to be in the future, and picks his stocks, bonds, and so on in hopes that his investments will take him there.

The big differences in their trading patterns reflect their widely divergent points of view. Over time, investors like Harry almost always emerge as the winners. But this doesn't bother Tom, as long as he gets a rush of excitement every now and then from a big gainer.

Tom knows what he wants, but he doesn't have what I would call investment aims or goals. Harry has investment aims, but he's not going about achieving them in the most effective way by actively picking stocks. I'll have more to say about this later.

Taking Action

You have to take action. You should never just drift into retirement, handling each crisis as it comes. But it's easy to say, "Take action." How exactly do you go about it? Obviously, each individual's circumstances are different and require appropriate steps. But, in general, you should follow these six courses of action:

1. **Adopt a disciplined and logical investment strategy.** This means relying on something other than emotions, hunches, and personal interests and biases for making investment decisions. Easier to say than do.

2. **Be constantly aware of what you don't know.** In other words, always wonder why you are the only one who sees the opportunity or lack of danger in something.

3. **Match your investments to your aims and risk tolerance.** To do this, you need to be sure of your investment aims and how much stress you are willing to undergo.

4. **Portfolio structure and diversification.** Asset allocation principally determines results in a broadly diversified portfolio, and diversification is the answer to uncertainty.

5. **Monitor and rebalance your portfolio regularly** Markets change and you must monitor and rebalance your portfolio to ensure your investment plan stays on course to meet your needs.

6. **Find a licensed financial advisor who you can trust.** The previous five steps should have already convinced you of the need for professional advice.

Chapter Two

Financial Upside

People who have been successful in their business or profession for decades often see things in terms of their work rather than in financial terms. When they retire, although sophisticated in the ways of the world, they can be somewhat at a loss in financial dealings outside the context of what they have done all their lives.

Some avoid coming to terms with this at any cost. Others resort to intense self-education. The smart ones find a good financial advisor.

What surprises most successful people is how little they actually understand about the upside of money. When they are in the accumulation phase of their lives, financial success is often less important than fulfilling their potential. The rewards can come later.

Later, when the rewards come, they may be taken almost for granted. Only upon retirement do many people view their finances as an independent entity. Like an ocean, their financial state can be deceptively calm.

The upside of money is how wealth grows, providing an enjoyable lifestyle and security for an individual or family. It usually involves steady accumulation over time.

The downside is loss and all that it entails. Loss may be sudden. We balance one against the other when we consider the financial risk of something. As we become more experienced in life, most of us become more skilled in evaluating such risk. We become so skilled, in fact, we may become risk averse—missing out on opportunities because we overweigh the negative side of the scales. On the other hand, too much caution can become a virtue in retirement.

In retirement, you obviously have fewer chances of financial recuperation than you had mid-career. If you have ideas, you need a sounding board now more than ever before. If you are undecided, you need professional advice. We look at investment risk in Chapter 4.

In this short chapter, I want to call your attention to how quickly money can accumulate when permitted to do so. Usually this is through compound interest. The power of compound interest can best be illustrated by some examples.

People can retire with a million dollars at age 65 if they invest the monthly amount shown in the chart in a tax-deferred fund at 9 percent, the monthly amount increasing with the age at which the investment is begun.

Age	Values up to Age 65
25	$46,030 (initial investment)
34	$92,016
43	$183,940
52	$367,697
61	$735,029
65	$1,000,000

Beyond age 45, tax laws limiting contributions may prevent you from accumulating a million dollars by age 65. Although it may be too late for you to participate in this program, perhaps you can interest your children or other younger family members in it. The numbers certainly show the potential of small investments over time.

Consider investing at birth on behalf of a grandchild. If you make a lump sum investment of $4,000 in a tax-deferred fund at an average annual return of 9 percent, he or she will have more than a million at the age of 65—and, no doubt, many warm memories of you!

Making the investment at birth requires the lowest sum. If your child or grandchild is, say, 25 years old, to provide him or her a million dollars by age 65, you can make a one-time investment of $46,030 in a trust earning 8 percent compounded annually. The money will accumulate as shown in the table.

Age Begun	Per Month	Per Year *(Value @ Age 65 $1,000,000)*
20	$136	$1,902
25	$214	$2960
30	$340	$4,636
35	$547	$7,337
40	$892	$11,807
45	$1,498	$19,547

Even When the Total Is Right …

I have been quoting numbers in these examples, but let me caution you not to be too hasty about making an investment just because the calculations look good on paper. Sometimes the numbers don't tell the whole story.

A clever marketer can put a spin on a presentation by choosing the financial statistics. Averages, in particular, are usually worth scrutinizing. They can be mathematically truthful but at the same time highly misleading.

For example, basing a decision solely on average annual returns can be risky. Because an investment has an average annual return of 10 percent over the past 5 years does not mean that it returned more or less 10 percent each year. In a highly negative example, the returns might have been:

Year 1: 40 percent
Year 2: 25 percent
Year 3: -5 percent
Year 4: -5 percent
Year 5: -5 percent
Average annual return: 10 percent

In this case, the seemingly healthy 10 percent average annual return over the past five years hides an ugly picture of persistent loss in value.

It's also worth keeping in mind that the compounding of money works in both directions. Losses can be compounded through the same process as gains. For example, take this 4-year sequence in which 3 years of 10 percent gains are followed by 1 year of a 10 percent loss:

Year 1: $1,000 gains 10 percent = $1,100
Year 2: $1,100 gains 10 percent = $1,210
Year 3: $1,210 gains 10 percent = $1,331
Year 4: $1,331 loses 10 percent = $1,197

This compression of returns has brought the total back below its year 2 level. Thus, a 10 percent loss for 1 year may not be equivalent to or reversed by a 10 percent gain the following year. It is another illustration of the adage that money accumulates slowly but can be lost quickly.

Doubling Your Money with Compound Interest
The way compound interest increases your original investment, even at single-digit interest rates, can be a pleasant surprise. For fast calculation, you can use the "rule of 72."

To see how many years it takes to double your original investment, divide the annual interest rate you are earning into 72. The result is approximately how many years it would take to double your money. This rule, of course, does not take into consideration withdrawals, taxes, or inflation, but does show the power of compounding.

At an annual rate of 9 percent, for example, it takes only 8 years (72 divided by 9) to double your money.

You may have noticed that my discussion of the financial upside has not included any big bets on stocks, financial windfalls, or get-rich-quick schemes—only the accumulation of money that has been allowed to increase over time.

Let your money grow. In most cases during retirement, you probably have no justifiable need to take on high risks. Enjoy life. Let a trusted financial advisor look after your money. And let your money look after you.

CHAPTER THREE

Market Price Reflects Reality

The prices of your assets rise or fall according to their market value. The closer you come to the financial market itself, the more intense the scrutiny from everyone involved. We've come a long way from the days when men traded in the shade of a big tree on Wall Street.

Today, it is my belief that the financial market is efficient. By this, I mean it quickly responds to supply and demand, with prices reflecting the latest information and judgment of investors. Thus, market prices, when free from rigging or manipulation, are fair to both buyers and sellers.

This is part of what is known as the *Efficient Market Hypothesis.* Academic work in this area is often referred to as *Modern Portfolio Theory,* which the American Law Institute made use of for its prudent investing guidelines for trust fiduciaries.

When the market isn't efficient for some reason, it can be argued that you have no reliable way to judge prices. Are they too high or too low? To have enough confidence to make a purchase in the market, you need some kind of assurance that the price you pay is what other buyers are paying.

With the arrival of computers in the mid-1960s, data on stocks, bonds, and mutual funds could be compared in ways never before possible. Prices came to depend on up-to-date and verifiable information. With readily available and easily used information, it became much harder to manipulate markets.

In recent decades, Securities and Exchange Commission (SEC) vigilance has also been responsible to a great degree for healthy American financial markets. Investors can assume that this federal agency's oversight and regulation help keep the playing field more or less level. In America today, we rightly take it for granted that prices reflect reality.

Stock Pickers Looking for Mispriced Stocks

My belief in an efficient market doesn't imply that I think the financial market is perfect in its efficiency. Far from it! A totally predictable market that operated like clockwork would leave almost no room for insightful and courageous investors to maneuver. There would be hardly any active "stock pickers."

Those who actively pick stocks today believe that the market is at least inefficient enough to make the search for the imperfections worthwhile. They search for stocks they consider to be worth more than the current prices assigned to them by the market and expect these market "mistakes" to be acknowledged by higher prices at a future date. Or, they search for stocks priced too high and sell short.

They pay the costs involved in discovering mispriced stocks, bonds, market sectors, and even whole markets. If and when they are proven right, they win. But, as experienced and knowledgeable professionals are acutely aware, studies have shown that the market is too efficient to allow them to overcome consistently the costs of picking mispriced stocks.

Many who play the stock market don't take these professionals into account. If they talked to them face to face, they might not be so willing to dispute the price the market assigns to a particular stock. In reality, they are disputing the price when they buy with an expectation that the price will change upward in the near future.

But you can be lucky. A discipline of professional gamblers is to maximize gains when on a winning streak, and minimize losses when losing steadily. That is, make big bets when you are on a roll, and don't play every hand when Lady Luck is keeping her distance.

This is often the approach of people who regard themselves as smart investors. Like many gamblers, they selectively remember their big wins and don't recall their steady losses.

When You Must Do Something
A person or couple can work hard for many years and suddenly find themselves, upon retirement, with a larger than usual amount of cash on hand and disposable assets that they have to wisely utilize for their future well being.

It's a tragedy when they lose much of their assets through their lack of knowledge of the financial marketplace. Unfortunately, this happens quite frequently. It happens regularly to people who have been making successful decisions over many years in a business or profession that they know inside and out. They have the self-confidence to make big decisions in an area they know little about.

It can be hard for, say, an eminent cardiac surgeon to acknowledge, even to himself, that he's unqualified to do what millions of ordinary people do. Some believe they can turn their hands to anything and make a success of it in less time than anyone else.

You don't meet many people with these attitudes who are full-time professionals in financial markets and services. The marketplace quickly cuts people down to size. Wall Street is filled with humbled people!

My advice is to forget looking for the stock that's going to streak ahead of others in the home stretch. Forget trying to find the great little stock that's only now coming into its own. Go to the track instead—or a casino, if you prefer. There, at least, you won't find it so easy to kid yourself about what you're doing.

Some call it gambling. You can call it speculating. But it's always important to remember that you're very likely to hurt yourself when you make investments in the same emotional way that you make bets.

Now that you're retiring, you may have to do something with your cash and assets in a relatively short time frame. Since I don't recommend trying to pick winners in the stock market, what have I to suggest?

I say invest, but don't assume that you can pick winners over losers. You don't have to spend all your energy trying to find big winners if you take a different approach to investing. In the next few chapters, you will see why this different approach works and how you can make use of it.

Your Money and Active Managers

When asked, most investors say that the fundamental rule in picking stocks is to buy low and sell high. But how can you tell whether a stock price is high or low? Can you really time the market?

It has been shown over and over that stocks can't be picked consistently, yet this is what active money managers try to do. They are known as active because they actively search for stocks that they believe have been mispriced by the market. When people hand over their investment money to active managers, they are implicitly stating their belief that mispriced stocks can be picked consistently, and if not by them, then by the managers.

While some active managers buy stocks for individual portfolios, others work as advisors to the average retail mutual funds. These mutual fund managers actively try to find mispriced stocks to put in the mutual fund portfolio.

Many people do not fully understand this active concept as it applies to mutual funds. They believe that a mutual fund provides diversification in that its shareholders do not own individual stocks. This is partially true, because the shareholders are allowed to own many stocks bundled within the mutual fund portfolio, but an active philosophy is being applied by the mutual fund manager.

Against all the evidence, we tend to accept the existence of investment superstars who can do what regular money managers and investors can't. We suppose they may have greater abilities or may work harder, but whatever it takes, these superstars succeed where others fail. They may be impressive on TV personal finance shows and have a gift for self-promotion.

But, for the most part, they are media creations. In the real financial marketplace, I would argue, they don't exist! There are no "real" superstars out there working to help other investors. If they themselves could pick stocks, they would do so and become multibillionaires—instead of appearing on talk shows and writing newsletters to tell us how to do it.

When the market is efficient, as we believe it normally is, a stock's price correctly reflects its value. Few mispriced stocks exist for an active fund manager or independent investor to profit from. For an active manager to be successful, as I said, the market has to fail by mispricing a stock.

That's what they mean on TV shows when they say a particular stock or market is overvalued or undervalued. In other words, the market got it wrong and they know the correct price. If they buy the stock at the present price, when the market moves from the incorrect to the correct price, they can sell and keep the price difference as a profit. The fact that the market doesn't get the price wrong very often is the problem with active stock picking.

I'm not disrespecting active fund managers. Many are very smart, very well educated, and very hard working. They need to be, since they're looking for something that's quite rare. You can even sympathize with an active manager whose task is to find enough imperfections in the market to yield, after transaction costs and taxes, a positive return.

It simply is very difficult to accomplish on a consistent basis. Take the world's greatest fisherman to a dry lake and he won't catch any fish. That's the challenge for an active manager in an efficient market.

How many mispriced stocks could a typical active manager running a mutual fund expect to find in a year? One, five, a dozen? Finding as many as twelve mispriced stocks in a single year sounds incredible to me. So what do active managers do?

Many have hundreds of stocks in their portfolios. If they were picking only mispriced stocks, I believe they would have far fewer holdings. The only explanation I can think of for holding hundreds of stocks is that these active stock pickers are hedging their bets through diversification. TV talk shows are one thing, but financial survival is another.

Passive Investing and Index Funds

While I have been speaking of my personal business experiences, I'm not suggesting that the conclusions about the efficient market and difficulty of picking stocks consistently are my own. In fact, Harry Markowitz, James Tobin, William Sharpe, and Paul Samuelson have all won the Nobel Prize in economics for academic work in this general area relating to investing.

I could name at least a half dozen other economists who deserve and may be awarded this prize in the next few years for similar work. What I have to say is based on market phenomena that these economists were the first to recognize and describe. In fact, at Liberty Asset Management, we are proud to claim that our investment philosophy is based solidly on the principles formulated by these Nobel winners and other eminent economists.

If you can't reliably forecast stock prices, how can you invest responsibly or successfully? That's a fair question. You can probably invest profitably if you know something about an industry or activity that is not known in the general marketplace. Not many of us, however, have this special kind of knowledge. We depend on the marketplace for our information.

An ingenious solution to this problem hit the stock market in 1971, with the arrival of passive index funds based on the Standard & Poor's 500 Index of major firms.

A fund is *passive* when the investors don't actively pick the stocks involved. Putting money into funds based on the S&P 500 Index is investing in a wide array of big companies, which is equivalent to investing in the entire stock market for this particular asset class (more on asset classes later). In contrast, the Dow Jones Industrial Average is a price-weighted average of 30 leading industrial stocks traded on the New York Stock Exchange.

When the market rises, you win. When it falls, you lose. In 1975, the New York Telephone Company invested $40 million, the first big investment in an S&P 500 Index fund.

Although index funds are seeing increased competition from more recently devised investing concepts (such as ETFs), they are seen as the big breakthrough in providing investors with a passive rather than active investment strategy.

Instead of rolling the dice with the uncertainties of individual companies, investors can now put their money on the entire broader market. Since the stock market is so important to the nation's economic well being, investing in it is much the same as placing a bet on America!

Confessions of a Superstar

In 1993, after he had retired from the Magellan Fund, Peter Lynch claimed that amateur stock picking was a dying art, because it could not compete against mutual funds. But the fact that three out of four mutual funds failed to perform even as well as the stock market averages showed that the money managers in charge of them were no geniuses.

Working out of Boston, Lynch himself was one of the biggest Wall Street celebrity money managers. He pointed out that amateur stock pickers, with discipline and common sense, could beat the star money managers most of the time.

The hard part for individual stock pickers, of course, is discipline and common sense. Most of us have more common sense about other people's investment behavior than our own. And few of us have the discipline to invest unemotionally.

Bad news is in endless supply: war, irresponsible political leaders, weather. Markets fall and we sell off when we should be buying. Lynch showed that people, even schoolchildren, who invested steadily and ignored or were ignorant of world affairs did better than those who tried to forecast what the market would do in response to the latest upheavals.

Lynch's solution was to rely on discipline and common sense as an individual stock picker. For the majority of investors, who lack Lynch's talent, experience, and other personal resources, this is no easy path to riches. It's even harder today, with increasingly high tech stock markets and instantly accessible accurate information, to find stocks that have been incorrectly priced by the full-time professionals.

In this chapter, I have mentioned diversification a few times. In the next chapter, we will look at how diversification can be your most effective way to lower investment risk. We will also see how asset allocation can be viewed as the best way to achieve diversification.

CHAPTER FOUR

Reducing Investment Risk

We often hear that nothing in life is without risk. Nothing ventured, nothing gained—and you can probably add a few more similar sayings. We have all heard about various kinds of risks. This is nothing new.

You need to assess the risk in something and then decide if the promised gain is worth the possible loss. To act without making that calculation would be reckless.

In your working life, you probably made risk assessments as second nature and, without giving them a lot of thought, undertook the calculated risks that "came with the territory."

In retirement, however, our economic roles change for most of us. We become investors rather than business people or professionals who also accumulate assets on the side. In retirement, managing what you already have—avoiding loss—is likely to become more important than further accumulation of assets. You need the viewpoint of an investor. You need to ask, should I be doing this?

Kinds of Investment Risk

To assess the risk of an investment, it helps to be aware of the different kinds of investment risk. Here are ten familiar kinds. You may already know them by the same or different names from your working life. Their order here does not indicate any greater likelihood of occurrence.

Market Risk

The returns from securities rise and fall in unpredictable ways with market conditions. Markets are affected by such things as recessions, tax law changes, armed conflicts, consumer preferences, and structural changes in the economy. These are often unpredictable events, and the degree to which securities markets react to them is often equally unpredictable.

Interest Rate Risk

The prices of securities generally move in the opposite direction to interest rate changes. Bonds are usually affected more strongly than stocks. As interest rates rise, bond prices fall, particularly when the interest rate becomes higher than the rate a bond pays.

Inflation Risk

The risk that the purchasing power of your invested money will decline is known as inflation risk. Since lenders ask for higher payments to make up for the loss in purchasing power, inflation risk is tied to interest rate risk. Stocks tend to rise in price faster than the inflation rate, outpacing inflation better than bonds or Treasury bills.

Regulation Risk

Investments having tax advantages, such as municipal bonds, are particularly vulnerable to changes in tax laws or regulations. If the tax exemption is lost, much of the security's value may be as well. In extreme cases, a security's liquidity may be threatened.

Liquidity Risk

A liquid security is one that can be bought or sold without delay or financial sacrifice. Treasury bills have a high liquidity. Shares in private companies and the stock of small companies in emerging markets that are traded over the counter are often low in price because of their low liquidity.

Reinvestment Risk

Bonds often have a provision that their issuers can redeem or call them in—that is, buy them back for a predetermined price or their current market value. This is likely to happen when the interest rate falls below the rate of the bond. The investor then has to reinvest at a lower interest rate or higher price.

Credit or Default Risk

This is the risk that a security's issuer may not live up to the promises made to investors. This kind of risk is often associated with business risk.

Business Risk

This is the risk of doing business in a particular industry or environment. The economic problems of American airlines and car manufacturers are examples.

Exchange Rate Risk

International equity markets often are included in a broadly diversified portfolio. In such cases, the exchange rate and costs must be taken into consideration before the profit can be calculated, unless you intend to leave your investment money in that overseas currency area for a long term.

In recent years, this risk has been lessened by the declining dollar. The risk of political instability has been of greater concern to international investors.

Longevity Risk

Longevity risk relates to the possibility of outliving your financial resources. This is becoming a statistical nightmare as life expectancies in America and other developed countries increase progressively on an annual basis.

As well as running out of money to meet daily living expenses, people foresee the possibility of having Alzheimer's disease or some other age-related infirmity that could make further demands on their already overextended financial resources.

Lessening Risk Through Diversification

The old saying of not putting all your eggs in one basket underlies today's best investment strategy for reducing risk. This strategy, known as diversification, can be your best friend in reducing volatility in a portfolio. The strategy is simple—in fact, it had been used without thought by investors for years before being studied by academicians.

Diversification can be seen at many levels, from simple to highly complex. For example, all the shares Alice owned were in Walgreen Company. She liked the company and had no particular concern about its future, but she didn't like all her eggs in one basket.

So, she sold some Walgreen shares and invested in CVS and Rite Aid. She knew their stores and felt comfortable with owning the companies' shares. Now, if something happened to Walgreen, she could fall back on them. She had diversified.

But Alice had only diversified in a limited way. She had stayed within her zone of comfort, which happened to be retail drug companies. If the entire retail drug sector of the stock market lost value, her limited diversification would not protect the total amount she had invested. To reduce her risk effectively, Alice needed to diversify beyond retail drug stocks.

Like Alice, most of us tend to buy stocks in areas of interest to us. Indeed, you see frequent counseling to invest only in what you know. But if all you know is baseball, you should not limit your investments to that area.

Likewise, investing all your money in the company you work for is not advisable—it can even have tragic consequences, as we have been hearing about in some big court cases.

Obviously, many kinds of stock exist and there are different ways to categorize them. Table 1 shows 10 broad categories of the 500 stocks in the S&P 500 index, according to the *Wall Street Journal*. Each category comprised the percentage of the index shown here in early March 2006. Because the numbers are rounded, the percentages do not total 100 percent.

Table 1. S&P 500 index categories

CATEGORY	Percent of Index
Financials	21
Technology	15
Healthcare	13
Industrials	11
Consumer discretionary	10
Consumer staples	9
Energy	9
Utilities	3
Materials	3
Telecommunications	3

With this wide array of stocks to choose from, there can be little justification for putting all your money into one kind of economic activity. There are far more stock categories than 10, of course, as you can readily see from the quarterly market reports published in the financial sections of newspapers.

If these categories mean little to you, you need the services of a professional financial advisor (see Chapter 9). Such an advisor can give you valuable guidance in choosing how to diversify your investments and lower your risk. But the selection of investments and amounts should reflect your aims and needs, and not be the one-size-fits-all formula.

Diversification and Asset Allocation

In the early 1950s, economist Harry Markowitz focused attention on diversification as a risk reduction strategy. Although diversification can also increase investment income, its chief attraction for investors has been its lowering of risk.

Markowitz, who was awarded the 1990 Nobel Prize in economics, developed the concept that you should be concerned with what is happening in your portfolio rather than in the market. He saw that an investor's properly balanced portfolio need not take a downturn just because the market did. The fall of some kinds of investments in such a portfolio could be offset by the rise of other kinds.

This led to the study of asset classes, which can be thought of as groups of securities with shared economic traits. The average price movements of asset classes are distinct and independent of each other. In a well-structured portfolio, the asset classes are balanced against one another to reduce the investor's risk.

Familiar examples of asset classes include large cap stocks, small cap stocks, international stocks, long-term government bonds, intermediate-term government bonds, and Treasury bills. Investors who hold all six of these or similar asset classes in a properly structured portfolio are clearly less vulnerable to market ups and downs than investors who have bet everything on a few hot stocks.

The nomenclature of asset classes varies somewhat with different advisors. Table 2 shows the asset classes used in many portfolios managed by our firm.

Table 2. Asset classes used in many portfolios.

Large Cap
Large Cap Value
Micro Cap
Small Cap
Real Estate Securities (REITs)
International Value
International Small Cap
International Small Cap Value
Emerging Markets
Emerging Markets Value
Emerging Markets Small Cap
Fixed income (bonds) part of portfolio:
One-Year Fixed Income Portfolio
Two-Year Global Fixed Income Portfolio
Five-Year Government Portfolio
Five-Year Global Fixed Income Portfolio

Before buying a stock, an advisor decides which asset class the stock belongs to and whether the portfolio needs another member of that asset class. In other words, the advisor manages by asset class rather than by star performing individual stocks.

I am not suggesting that investors start working on asset allocation, which is the term used for balancing asset classes in a portfolio. If you already have this kind of knowledge, use it. If not, find someone you can trust who is knowledgeable.

Investors only need to know what's involved and that they are benefiting from the strategy. It is our belief at Liberty Asset

Management that asset allocation is the most effective means known to achieve diversification and thereby reduce risk.

The Dow Jones Industrial Average is one of the best-known yardsticks of how stocks are doing on Wall Street, but it is not a measurement of asset classes, since it only tracks 30 of the largest public companies. The Russell 2000 Index tracks smaller companies, and the Russell Microcap Index tracks the smallest companies.

Size matters. For example, when the dollar is weak, big (large cap) companies are more likely to benefit than smaller (small cap) companies, because big companies are more likely to be exporters and own overseas divisions. They are also more likely to benefit from rising interest rates because they have better access to credit and stronger balance sheets than small cap companies.

On the other hand, in an economy emerging from a recession, small cap companies are more likely to have speedier returns to profit than slower-moving, large cap companies.

Table 3 shows the 14 asset classes used by the *Wall Street Journal* in its mutual funds monthly review.

Table 3. Asset classes used by the Wall Street Journal to classify mutual funds.

Large Cap Core	Small Cap Core
Large Cap Value	Small Cap Value
Large Cap Growth	Small Cap growth
Midcap Core	Multicap Core
Midcap Value	Multicap Value
Midcap Growth	Multicap Growth
Gold Oriented	Latin American Funds

Practical Approach to Asset Allocation

Knowledge and judgment are essential in structuring a portfolio. You need to know the various asset classes and judge how they behave in comparison to each other.

You can reduce this practical approach to three elements: (1) the performance history of asset classes, (2) the risk history of asset classes, and (3) the comparative performance of asset classes. We'll look very briefly at each.

Performance History of Asset Classes
Different asset classes vary widely in their returns. Understanding just how widely they can vary is obviously important in asset allocation (Tables 4 and 5). Small cap stocks tend to provide the highest return of any asset class.

Table 4. How much $1 invested in four asset classes in 1925 would be worth in mid 2003. With inflation, $1 in 1925 equals $10 in 2003.

Asset Class	1925	Mid-2003
Small cap stocks	$1	$8,300
Large cap stocks	$1	$2,659
Core bonds	$1	$72
Treasury bills	$1	$19

SOURCE: Wilshire Associates

It's worth noting in Table 5 that the annualized return over an extended period is only rarely the actual return in any given year. In other words, you can't use this table to predict the annual return for an asset class next year.

Table 5. Annualized return for 6 asset classes.

Asset Class	Annualized Return (1926-2002), Percent
Small cap stocks	12.2
Large cap stocks	10.2
International stocks (1970-2002)	10.1
Long-term government bonds	5.5
Intermediate-term government bonds	5.4
Treasury bills	3.8

SOURCE: Ibbotson Associates

Looking at returns alone, it might seem reasonable to invest all your money in small cap stocks. It might be, were it not for the risk.

Risk History of Asset Classes

The more risk, the higher the return. Those selling riskier stocks usually have to offer a higher rate of return to attract investors. Another generalization has it that risky stocks are more suitable for younger, rather than older, investors.

Certainly, you have to figure that losses during retirement are less likely to be recouped. On retirement, most investors are willing to accept lower returns on investments in exchange for lower risk. This is in line with what I recommend: first and foremost, hold on to what you have. You can best do this by reducing risk.

Thus, asset allocation will most likely differ greatly for someone with 30 years of working life ahead than for someone entering retirement. The younger person's investment mix will probably reflect a greater acceptance of risk in exchange for higher returns. The retiring person's asset allocation will likely have avoidance of loss as its primary aim.

One way to reduce risk is to make use of fixed-income securities (bonds) and cash. But their low rates of return, relative to stocks, need to be taken into consideration. Just how much of a return is an individual investor willing to sacrifice in exchange for lowering risk?

Each investor has his or her own level of risk tolerance, as well as his or her own need for investment income. A well-structured portfolio is built to be responsive to its owner's characteristics.

You can use standard deviation to measure the amount of risk inherent in an asset class. The standard deviation is the percentage variation in return that you can expect two-thirds of the time.

For example, an asset class with an expected 10 percent return and a 1-year standard deviation of 5 percent would have, 67 percent of the time, a return between 10 + 5 = 15 percent and 10 – 5 = 5 percent.

Table 6 shows the standard deviation and annualized long-term return for 5 asset classes, from the most volatile (small cap stocks) to the least volatile (Treasury bills).

Table 6. Risk performance of 5 asset classes over time.

Asset Class	Standard Deviation, Percent	Annualized Return (1926-2002), Percent
Small-cap stocks	33.2	12.2
International stocks (1970-2002)	22.6	10.1
S&P 500 index	20.5	10.2
Long-term government bonds	9.4	5.5
Treasury bills	3.2	3.8

SOURCE: Ibbotson Associates

Comparative Performance of Asset Classes

Modern portfolio theory is used in combining various asset classes to manage risk and return. The ideal for each investor is a portfolio that gives the highest possible return at the level of risk at which that investor is comfortable.

Put very simply, your portfolio should be structured from asset classes that move in price independently of each other and not always in the same direction. In other words, when some asset classes drop in market price, others rise, maintaining the overall value of the portfolio.

When assets (such as stocks or mutual funds) tend to move together in the same direction, they are said to have positive correlation. An example of this is the S&P 500 and Dow Jones Industrial Average index funds. Both are made up of the stock of American large cap companies and thus are likely to move up or down in price simultaneously. Because of this, they don't provide effective diversification.

Adding assets with negative correlation to each other is more desirable, because they tend to move in price in opposite directions, providing portfolio diversification. American stocks and bonds used to move in opposite directions in predictable ways, but as mentioned earlier, their opposed movements have become less predictable. Foreign stocks often have negative correlation with long-term government bonds.

The aim is to avoid creating a portfolio with assets that move in the same price direction with market changes. Using different asset classes with negative correlation provides for more effective portfolio diversification.

Efficient Portfolios

There seems to be no limit to the number of asset class combinations that can provide portfolio diversification. When the combination of classes in a portfolio delivers the maximum return at the acceptable risk level, the portfolio is known as efficient.

Efficient portfolios exist along what is called the *efficient frontier.* Portfolios on either side of the efficient frontier have either insufficient returns or too much risk.

Generally speaking, the greater the degree of diversification or asset classes held in a portfolio, the better the opportunity for a successful investment experience without added risk. Thus, a portfolio is never complete—it can always be improved upon and added to.

It should come as no surprise that software programs are available to help investors with this. These programs are known as *optimizers.*

Efficient portfolios may use either strategic or tactical asset allocation. Strategic allocation is popular with investors in retirement because it stresses an unchanging approach and does not require constant attention.

Tactical allocation, on the other hand, involves changing the combinations of asset classes in a portfolio to take advantage of market opportunities.

From the above, you'll probably already have made the correct assumption that your portfolio will only be as efficient as your financial advisor is.

Play Money

A client of mine, a longtime stock picker during his working years, told me he was very happy with his efficient portfolio. All the same, he had one complaint: in his retirement, he missed the fun of playing the market.

He had no wish to put most of his assets at risk for the sake of excitement, but he suggested that we set aside $100,000 for him to use as play money. I think I surprised him by agreeing immediately. The fact that the amount involved was only a small part of his assets helped.

Since then, he lets me know every time he picks a winner.

CHAPTER FIVE

Monitoring and Rebalancing Your Portfolio

John prided himself on long-term planning and never veering "off-course." He was a strategic rather than tactical investor. His financial advisor built an efficient portfolio for him in the mid 1990s, with an initial allocation comprised of 60 percent stocks, 30 percent bonds, and 10 percent money funds. This was the asset allocation his advisor recommended given John's risk tolerance and desired level of return.

John often commented that his advisor was being too rigid and that he was missing big opportunities in the booming stock market. His advisor agreed but encouraged John to let the opportunities go in favor of retaining the 60:30:10 asset mix.

Frequently, the advisor had to sell highly appreciated stocks continually to keep the portfolio's equity allocation at its target level of 60 percent. John often watched as his advisor sold climbing *high tech* and *large cap* stocks. He sometimes argued and pleaded with his advisor not to sell the soaring stocks, but his advisor convinced him of the importance of remaining disciplined.

When the high tech bubble burst in early 2002, John was hurt—but not nearly to the extent of investors who had over-loaded their portfolios with high-performing tech stocks. By keeping to his asset mix, he had limited his exposure to these assets and sold off nothing at a loss when the market crashed. Within six months, his portfolio value had recovered and he had a new found respect and appreciation for his advisor.

Three things could be responsible for John's successful weathering of this storm: he and his advisor had established his risk tolerance, they had a strategy that took it into account, and his advisor made him stick to it. His advisor convinced him to stay with that strategy even when it was costing him opportunities in the market.

This was the price he had to pay to keep his investment risk at a level acceptable to him. Such clear and uncomplicated thinking is a characteristic of many successful investors and their advisors. They know what they want, they know how to get it, and they stay on course.

Monitoring Your Portfolio
Because markets are always changing with supply and demand, as well as reacting in various ways to unpredictable events, your assets need constant herding.

Financial professionals can usually monitor assets better than investors can, since they are more likely to be plugged into impor-tant information networks and objective about what they hear. You just can't leave your assets out to pasture and forget about them—unless of course you have someone you can trust to ride herd on them.

Monitoring assets normally centers around keeping risk at an acceptable level and ensuring that income is being produced. "Rebalancing" is the term used for any adjustments that return a portfolio to the acceptable level of risk.

In a Lipper Analytical study, failure to monitor and rebalance resulted, over a 3-year period, in a portfolio's value base moving from 60 percent stocks and 40 percent bonds to 41 percent stocks and 59 percent bonds. No value was lost, but the exposure to risk was changed significantly.

In fact, after only three years, the risk exposure was exactly opposite to what it was when the portfolio began. This is what can result without monitoring and, needless to say, it creates the potential for an unpleasant surprise. Monitoring should take place at least quarterly.

Rebalancing: Time to Take Your Profit
Rebalancing can help lower your risk by reducing the volatility of stocks in your portfolio.

Two identical hypothetical portfolios in a UBS Global Asset Management study were composed of 60 percent S&P 500 Index and 40 percent Lehman Treasury Index. One was rebalanced once a year for 20 years through the end of 2002, and the other was not rebalanced for the same period.

At the end of the 20 years, there was little variability in return between the two portfolios, with an average annual return of 10.99 percent for the un-rebalanced portfolio, and 10.92 for the rebalanced one. But, at the end of the period, there was a big variability in average annual downside risk between the two portfolios, with –15.04 percent for the un-rebalanced portfolio and –5.21 percent for the rebalanced one.

If rebalancing can reduce your portfolio risk each year by about 10 percent, it's an investment tool you can't afford to overlook!

Many investors are aware of the benefits of rebalancing but don't take advantage of it because of trading costs, which can be high if it requires a number of transactions. You need to pay attention to costs when rebalancing. However, they should not deter you from staying the course.

Rebalancing often involves selling big winners—"buy low, sell high," as they say. Rebalancing may very well be your best time to take profits. It's usually nearly impossible to say when a stock will be at its highest price and sell it then.

Sometimes you choose correctly. Just as often, the stock rises to unexpected new levels after you have sold it. When rebalancing sets the time of sale, you may discover that it is no more or less arbitrary than other methods, but at least has the benefit of reducing your risk.

Don't underestimate the vigilance and discipline it takes to monitor and rebalance a portfolio. It's hard to stick with your original strategy when new opportunities present themselves. It can be even harder to sell high-performing stocks. What do you replace them with? Losers? The answer is often yes.

For most of us, this goes against the grain. To understand and accept the reasoning involved is one thing, but to take action on logic alone may be quite another.

These emotions affect everyone. For example, professionals find it much easier to be objective about their clients' portfolios than their own—and they often make better decisions for their clients than for themselves.

In the next chapter, we will take a brief look at some of the assets you may hold, and in Chapter 9, we will consider what is involved in finding a good financial advisor.

CHAPTER SIX

An Overview of Assets

To truly diversify your investments, you need to go beyond simply owning stocks. A myriad of investment options exist, and although there's no need to become knowledgeable about all of them, it can help to know that they are there.

In the last few years, there has been a striking emergence of products tailored to investors' special needs. These range from customer-friendly mortgages with creative payment schedules to derivatives on the stock market designed to protect other investments.

The wide spectrum of choice may bewilder newcomers. I suggest that you bypass the complexity and, instead, concentrate on the personal path you wish to follow. When you know exactly what you want from your investments, a financial advisor can tell you the best way to get it. The clearer you are in your mind about your investment needs or aims, the more effective the advisor's advice is likely to be.

In this chapter, we take a quick look at of some of the assets you are likely to hold. You can skip the familiar parts. We begin with stocks and then move on to bonds, real estate, gold, and collectibles.

Because mutual funds are some of the most widely held investments, we'll give them their own Chapter (7), which also includes exchange-traded funds (ETFs).

Stocks

A share of stock is an ownership interest in a corporation, represented by a certificate that is sold to the public. The owner of *common stock* is entitled to dividends declared by the board of directors and has a vote at the annual shareholders meeting. The owner of *preferred stock* often has no vote and only gets reduced dividends, but has a priority claim to income from earnings and assets in the event of liquidation.

Convertible preferred stock can be converted at a later time to a certain number of common shares, sometimes at a conversion ratio of two or three to one. Although it costs more than common stock, convertible preferred stock usually pays a higher dividend and fluctuates less in price.

Holders of class A stocks may have more voting rights than holders of class B stocks. The partial ownership represented by a stock is called *equity,* and stocks themselves are often called *equities.*

Stocks come in many kinds. *Value stocks* tend to trade at lower prices relative to their fundamentals such as dividends, earnings, and sales. Their prices may be low because the companies operate in an economically depressed business or because the companies themselves are seen as not being well run. A change of circumstances could cause a change of fortune and an increase in price.

Blue chips—stocks issued by long-established, high-prestige companies—provide moderate income and are considered less risky. Their comparative lack of volatility attracts investors.

Franchise stocks (which have nothing to do with franchises) are blue chip stocks of monopolies and other companies that do well regardless of economic conditions. The problem with blue chips is their high purchase price.

High-yield stocks are often sought by investors who desire income at the expense of growth. They are generally considered dependable and typically pay dividends higher than the interest on a savings account, and thus are popular with people who choose steady income over growth in value.

Traditionally, utility company stocks belonged to this type, but more recently, their dividends have become less reliable. Preferred stocks may also pay high dividends. *Equity-income stocks* are common stocks that pay high dividends.

Growth stocks may be considered risky, depending on the company. With a growth stock, the company typically does not pay a dividend but puts the money back into the company to promote future growth. Investors buy this type of stock in hopes that it will appreciate in price with growth.

Small cap stocks provide less income and are generally considered to be riskier. Their capitalization (total value of outstanding shares) is generally less than $100 million and thus comparatively small.

When the companies are successful, their stocks often enjoy a greater degree of price appreciation. But investors need to consider carefully the risk associated with owning small caps.

Large cap stocks have a greater capitalization and more moderate risk. With company success, they may provide generous annual growth. Both small cap and large cap growth stocks are often viewed as being attractive for their potential growth in value, as compared to their dividend income.

Distressed or turnaround stocks are generally high risk and high income. Investors who specialize in them are often said to be bottom fishing, because the companies are usually more or less insolvent. These investors hope to profit from a business turnaround, company breakup, or bankruptcy settlement. This is mostly a field for highly knowledgeable investors.

Cyclical stocks are also oftentimes considered to possess characteristics of higher risk and high income. These stocks react to economic change; they rise or fall with changes in interest rates, gasoline prices, consumer spending, and so on. Stocks of companies associated with the auto and construction industries are well known examples. Cyclical stocks may be included in a portfolio when they meet the parameters of a particular asset class.

Penny stocks are generally priced at less than a dollar, and their prices are quoted in "pink sheets" among brokers rather than in the media. Their risks and values may be almost impossible to assess with any certainty.

IPOs (initial public offerings), also known as *new issues,* are stocks newly arriving on the market, usually issued by companies that have just gone public. There have been problems with favored clients of merchant banks receiving them at a modest price and reselling them for an instant profit.

Foreign stocks are usually sold in United States stock markets as American Depository Receipts (ADRs) rather than as stock. Their excellent performance over the past two decades has transformed them from exotic investments into regular staples for American investors. Foreign stocks do not necessarily move in the same price direction as their American counterparts.

Bonds

Generally speaking, a bond is a certificate of indebtedness that pays a fixed rate of interest over the life of the obligation and hence is known as a fixed-income security. The issuer is obligated by the written bond indenture to pay the holder a fixed interest rate, usually semiannually, plus the face or par value of the certificate at maturity. (In zero-coupon bonds, all payments are made at maturity.)

Bonds may be issued with maturities ranging from two to thirty years. Investors often stagger the maturities of the different bonds they hold in an approach called *laddering.*

You can use bonds to reduce the overall risk in your portfolio. They can also supply you with a reliable source of income. Many investors use them for both purposes.

When interest rates rise, a bond's fixed interest rate may become lower than the going market rate; this makes the bond less desirable and causes its price to drop. On the other hand, when interest rates fall, a bond's fixed rate has the opposite effect.

But instead of paying interest at higher than the market rate over an extended period, the bond issuer may "call" its bonds before maturity, meaning that the issuer pays what you are owed and cancels the bond. In reality, the issuer is refinancing the bond at a lower rate, just as a homeowner might do with a mortgage.

Before buying bonds, you should inquire whether the issuer has the right to do this and at what point. Some bond issuers promise not to call their bonds before a certain number of years.

Bonds, unlike stocks, confer no ownership rights on their holders. However, *convertible bonds* may be exchanged for preferred stock. Most convertibles are *debentures*—that is, unsecured promises to pay.

Before deciding whether to purchase a bond, you should first determine whether the prospective bond issuer will be able to meet its obligations. There are three main bond rating companies that can help you accpmplish this goal. The table below provides you with a brief overview of the ratings classifications for each agency.

Moody's Investors Service	Aaa to C
Standard & Poor's	AAA to D
Fitch Investor Service	AAA to D

An S&P rating of C means that a company may stop paying interest on its bonds, while a D rating means that the company is in default and not paying interest. Junk bonds typically have a rating of BB (or Ba) or lower.

In order to persuade investors to buy them, companies have to offer comparatively high interest rates. You then have to judge whether the company will be able to pay these high rates for the lifetime of the obligation and repay the debt at maturity. This kind of high-risk investing is usually not recommended for anyone in retirement.

Bonds come in different types. We will look at only a few of the major kinds here.

U.S. Treasury Bills, Notes, and Bonds

All U.S. Treasury securities are easy to buy and sell, and none have to be held to maturity. They are exempt from state and local but not federal taxes.

T-bills have a maturity of a year or less, T-notes of 1 to 10 years, and Treasury Bonds of 10 to 30 years. Government securities are not callable. You can thus depend on receiving a fixed interest rate for the lifetime of the debt. They can be bought directly at little or no cost or through banks, brokers, or employers at minimal fees.

The lowest denomination of T-bills is $10,000, and they have a lifetime of 3, 6, or 12 months. You buy the T-bill at a discount and receive the face value at maturity.

T-notes and Treasuries have a lowest denomination of $1,000 and can be bought directly or through brokers. Although they, like T-bills, are sold at a discount and are redeemed at face value at maturity, they are traded on the market like corporate bonds, with changing daily yields and prices.

U.S. Savings Bonds come in two series: EE and HH. Series EE bonds, like T-bills, are sold at a discount and are redeemable at face value at maturity. If you sell them before maturity, their price will reflect this. There's no commission for buying or selling these bonds, although there is a penalty for cashing them in before five years elapse.

Series HH bonds can only be purchased with matured Series EE bonds. You pay face value for Series HH bonds and receive interest payments semiannually. By rolling over matured series EEs into HH bonds, you can defer federal taxes until the HH bonds mature.

Ginnie, Fannie, and Friends

The federal government helps first-time homebuyers and the home mortgage industry in general through cash infusions from bonds issued by three federal agencies.

These bonds have colorful popular names: Ginnie Mae (from the Government National Mortgage Association), Fannie Mae (from the Federal National Mortgage Association), and Freddie Mac (from the Federal Home Loan Mortgage Corporation). Because they have higher risk levels than Treasury securities, they generally pay a higher interest rate.

Federal agencies provide backing for education through two bonds: Sallie Mae (from the Student Loan Marketing Association) and Connie Lee (from the College Construction Loan Insurance Association).

Collateral Backed Securities

These are often asset-backed securities, such as mortgage-backed securities, in which many assets may be bundled. Their maturities and yields vary widely, as do their asset mixes. Some are pools of Ginnie Mae, Fannie Mae, and Freddie Mac bonds. Others consist of large numbers of home mortgages bundled by mortgage brokers or banks. This is a field for knowledgeable investors.

Municipal Bonds

Municipal bonds (munis) are exempt from federal income tax. In most states, they are exempt from state and local taxes for resident investors.

Munis are issued by state and local government agencies and usually have lower yields than corporate bonds. They appeal mainly to people in a high federal tax bracket and those who have high state or local taxes.

Munis come in two kinds: general obligation (GO) bonds and revenue bonds. GO bonds are backed by taxes and are the safer of the two. Revenue bonds are backed by the revenue to be generated by the state or local government project for which the bonds were issued.

Government issued munis can be moderately risky. Bankruptcies take place regularly, so don't assume that any state or federal guarantees exist. Munis may also be callable.

Zero-Coupon Bonds

Any bond sold at a discount and redeemable at face value at maturity is a zero-coupon bond. They are so called because no coupons are used to collect semiannual interest payments, as they are in interest-paying bonds.

A convenience of zero-coupon bonds is that they can be put away till maturity. Their drawbacks are that transaction-based brokers charge a commission on the face value rather than the discounted purchase price, and that taxes are due every year on income, even though the bonds are not sold.

Real Estate Investment Trusts (REITs)

Real estate investment trusts (REITs) own property, such as shopping centers, office buildings, and apartment buildings. Their stock trades on exchanges. A few mutual funds specialize in them, and well-managed REITs can prove to be valuable additions to a portfolio. However, efficient management is essential to their success.

Equity REITs buy, manage, and sell properties. Mortgage REITs specialize in financing rather than owning properties. And hybrid REITs do both.

Collateralized mortgage obligations (CMO) REITs are high-risk and ultra sensitive to interest rates. Finite life-equity REITs (FREITs) usually invest in an unchanging portfolio of properties with time-limited mortgages, often from 5 to 15 years. The FREIT is generally closed when the portfolio is exhausted, much as a limited partnership would be.

REITs attract investors because they generate income; they are required to pass on a high percentage of rent payments to shareholders and make large capital gains distributions. Unlike acquiring property, investors can commit comparatively small amounts of money, and get in and out at will.

Gold

The price of gold often moves counter to the stock market and this makes it a protective asset in a portfolio. In late February 2006, an ounce of gold cost $548 in commodities trading, near its 25-year peak.

Investors held more than 14 million ounces of gold in ETFs, equivalent to about one-quarter of the world's supplies in 2005. Few investors hold gold in the form of bars, secure storage being one problem. Some buy gold certificates or stock in gold mining companies. Most buy coins, which can be readily sold again.

Popular one-ounce gold bullion coins.

NAME	COUNTRY OF ORIGIN
Britannia	Great Britain
Eagle	United States
Krugerrand	South Africa
Maple Leaf	Canada
Nugget	Australia
Panda	China
Philharmoniker	Austria

Most popular gold coins contain about an ounce of gold. Dealers sell them at a small premium to the market price of their gold content. You generally will not get back this dealer's premium when you sell the coins.

For two or three popular Krugerrands, the premium is around six percent. For fewer or less popular coins, it is more.

Gold coins are best stored in a bank safety deposit box.

Collectibles

Collectibles have the greatest potential of all assets for gain or loss.

Consider rare gold coins as collectibles. An American $10 gold coin minted in 1799 contains only half an ounce of gold but sells for about $27,500. A 1787 gold coin known as the Brasher Doubloon sold in 2005 for $2.9 million, up from its 1981 auction value of $625,000.

In January 2006, a 1927 gold coin sold for $1.9 million, up from its $176,000 auction price in 1982. While this may sound crazy to some people, these sums and markups are reasonably modest in the world of collectibles.

In the decade ending in June 2005, the value of Old Master paintings rose 50 percent and contemporary art rose 55 percent, according to the British insurance underwriter Hiscox and Art Market Research.

"There was a time when you could not sell a painting in England unless it had a horse or a dog in it, preferably both," Robert Read of Hiscox told the *Financial Times*. "But now there has been a shift away from old furniture, silver and Old Masters."

If you understand these shifts, you know more than most investors. By all means, if you are interested and can afford them, purchase collectibles for your enjoyment. But be wary of purchasing them as assets that you expect to increase in value. Also, don't let your interest in items persuade you that a viable market exists for them.

In the next chapter, we will look at mutual funds, exchange-traded funds (ETFs), and some other investments.

CHAPTER SEVEN

Mutual Funds and ETFs

In this chapter, we look at investment companies that sell shares to investors. Mutual funds are the best known of these companies and get the most attention here.

Other kinds, much more briefly described, have special features that make them particularly desirable to some investors. They include closed-end funds, unit investment trusts (UITs), hedge funds, and exchange-traded funds (ETFs).

Mutual Funds

A mutual fund is an open-end investment company that invests its shareholders' money in stocks, bonds, government securities, or short-term money market instruments, as well as futures, options, or collectibles. An open-end investment company facilitates the entry and exit of shareholders.

Mutual fund shareholders own the securities in which the fund invests and pay taxes on income from the fund. The attraction of mutual funds is that they provide investors with diversification into perhaps hundreds of different stocks that are chosen by fund managers, usually without the requirement of investing large sums.

Mutual funds are not traded on exchanges. Shareholders make their money through the appreciation in value of their fund shares, dividends, and capital gains distributions.

The SEC emphasizes the following three points about mutual funds:

- An investment risk exists. Unlike bank deposits, mutual funds are not insured by the FDIC, even when issued by a bank.

- A mutual fund's past performance is not a reliable indicator of its future performance. Over time, however, a fund's past performance can be an indicator of its volatility.

- In all mutual funds, costs reduce your profits. Before you invest, compare the costs of various funds on the SEC website: www.sec.gov/investor/tools.shtml. See the section later in this chapter titled "Mutual Fund Costs."

You buy shares from the mutual fund company itself or from a broker representing the fund, and you sell back (redeem) the shares in the same way. The shares are not traded from investor to investor, like stock on the stock market. The price that you pay for a share is the mutual funds per share net asset value (NAV) plus the purchase fees (sales loads) the fund charges.

Mutual funds usually sell new shares on an ongoing basis, stopping only when a fund threatens to become unmanageably large. The investment portfolios of mutual funds are managed by financial advisors.

The advantages of mutual funds for individual investors are obvious. The securities that a mutual fund invests in are selected by professionals with skills, experience, and access to information. The large number of different stocks in the mutual fund portfolio may help you lower the risk level of your portfolio, even when the financial advisor is an active stock picker.

Many mutual funds permit you to invest modest amounts, often on a fixed schedule, which can be a very practical investment approach for wage earners. As well as affordability, most mutual funds provide liquidity, which means that you can quickly redeem your shares at their current NAV less any sales fees imposed by the fund.

These costs, which must be paid regardless of how a fund does, are a disadvantage of some mutual funds. In addition, bad timing in purchasing shares can leave you open to capital gains taxes (see later section titled "Mutual Fund Tax Consequences").

Another disadvantage to some investors is the lack of control over what specific stocks are bought or sold by the mutual fund. While you can choose one that focuses on certain types of stocks or securities (think asset allocation), you have no say in the particular securities held in the actual mutual fund portfolio.

Although mutual funds must recalculate their NAV at least once every business day, they often do so late in the day. Thus, the buying and selling prices of mutual fund shares are not available instantly like stock prices, and they do not rise and fall over the course of a single trading session as stock prices can.

Your return from mutual funds is generated in three ways: through dividends, capital gains distributions, and NAV increase.

- **Dividends.** The money that a mutual fund earns on its investments may be paid, less costs, to shareholders in the form of regular dividends.

- **Capital gains distributions.** When a mutual fund sells an asset at a profit, it has a capital gain. At year-end, a fund pays its shareholders a capital gains distribution made up of its capital gains less capital losses for the year.

• **NAV increases.** When the total value of a mutual fund's portfolio increases, this is reflected by a rise in its NAV— that is, an increase in its share value.

With mutual funds, you have the option of receiving your payments by check or reinvesting the money, often with no purchase commission.

Mutual Fund Types

The huge number of mutual funds available can look formidable to someone who has limited time in which to make a choice. But don't consider this a vast menu from which to make random or whimsical choices. Just because you can invest doesn't mean you should.

Keep your own investment aims in mind. What are you investing for? When will you need income from the investment? And what is your risk tolerance? Those three questions alone can help reduce the menu to a more manageable list of choices.

Mutual funds generally focus on a particular kind of investment, such as stocks or bonds. They can be easily categorized into three broad types: stock or equity funds, bond or fixed income funds, and money market funds. We now look briefly at each of the three types.

Stock or Equity Funds

Mutual funds that invest primarily in stocks have been the best performers over time, although they can be highly volatile over the short-term. They have a higher level of risk than either bond or money market funds.

Stock funds fit into the following general categories:

• **Growth funds** invest in stocks that have a potential for big capital gains, although they may not pay dividends regularly.

• **Value funds** invest in stocks considered to be under-priced by the market. When the market corrects this mispricing, the price of the stock rises, providing a return to the investor.

- **Income funds** concentrate on stocks with dependable high dividends, sometimes at the expense of growth. They often invest in government securities and utilities stocks.

- **Index funds** invest in all or a representative sample of the stocks that make up particular indexes, such as the S&P 500 Index.

- **Sector funds** invest in a particular industry or area of economic activity.

Smaller, special interest categories of stock funds include precious metals funds that invest mostly in gold, silver, and platinum; international funds that trade on foreign stock markets; lifecycle funds that come with a target retirement date and move to more conservative funds as investors age; and socially conscious or green funds that invest in the stocks of companies that embrace social or environmental principles.

There are also blended funds that invest in various asset classes such as stocks, bonds, and money markets and therefore allow an investor to diversify a portfolio by holding a single fund.

As indicated above, the list of mutual funds available to investors is quite extensive and it would be best for you to discuss your goals with a knowledgeable professional.

Bond or Fixed Income Funds

Bond funds—mutual funds that invest primarily in bonds—may specialize in short-term or long-term bonds, munis, mortgage-backed bonds, corporate bonds, or government securities. Shareholders of bond funds do not have to be concerned about the maturities of bonds in the fund and can cash out at any time without penalty.

Although bonds are often used to reduce the risk level of a portfolio, because they are less volatile and frequently move in a different price direction than stocks, bond funds are not risk free. The SEC cautions investors about the following three risks:

- **Credit risk** lies in the possibility that the bond issuer won't pay its debt. This kind of risk is highest in funds that specialize in corporate bonds issued by companies with poor credit ratings. It is minimal in funds that focus on insured bonds or U.S. Treasury bonds.

- **Interest rate risk** centers on the fact that when interest rates rise, bond prices fall. When this happens, you can lose money in any bond fund, including those that invest solely in insured bonds and Treasury bonds. Funds that specialize in longer term bonds have a higher interest rate risk.

- **Prepayment risk** occurs when interest rates fall beneath the rate paid by the bond. As mentioned earlier, the bond issuer may call the bond by paying off (retiring) its debt. This can deprive a fund of an important source of income.

Money Market Funds

These are mutual funds that invest in short-term debt instruments such as T-bills, high-quality corporate bonds, and negotiable certificates of deposit. These funds typically invest in low-risk bonds with maturities of 60 days or less.

The NAV of money market fund shares is usually $1.00, but a fund's poor performance can cause it to fall below this. Shareholders in money market funds are paid interest regularly. However, over longer periods of time, returns are generally lower than those of stock and bond funds and can be eroded by a rising inflation rate.

Mutual Fund Costs

Like all businesses, mutual funds have to pay their operating costs. Generally speaking, the higher a fund's costs, the lower your investment return. Although the percentages of these costs may appear negligible, their amounts can become sizable over time.

SEC regulations require the funds to disclose these costs in their prospectuses. Although methods and terminology vary among funds, they generally fall under the headings of either shareholder fees or operating expenses.

Shareholder Fees

- **Front-end sales load** is usually the broker's commission that you pay on purchasing fund shares. The maximum allowed is 8.5 percent. You need to deduct the amount from your total investment.

- **Purchase fee** is paid to the fund rather than a broker.

- **Back-end load** is usually the broker's commission that you pay on selling fund shares. It may be called a contingent deferred sales load (CDSL) or charge (CDSC). In many funds, when you hold shares for sufficient time, the back-end load decreases to zero.

- **Redemption fee** is paid to the fund rather than a broker on sale of shares.

- **Exchange fee** is charged by some funds for transfer of your investment from one fund to another within a group or family of funds.

- **Account fee** may be charged for account maintenance, particularly when your investment falls below a certain amount.

Operating Expenses

- **Management fee** is paid to the fund's financial advisor.

- **12b-1 fee,** named after an SEC rule, covers marketing and some administrative costs. It may be called a distribution fee or shareholder service fee.

- **Other expenses** are operating costs not included in either of the two categories above.

- **Expense ratio** is the total annual fund operating expenses expressed as a percentage of the fund's average net assets. You can use the expense ratio as a convenient way of comparing mutual fund costs.

No-load mutual funds do not charge a sales load, but they may charge other shareholder fees such as purchase, redemption, exchange, and account fees, as well as operating expenses. If these other costs are relatively high, the total costs of a no-load fund may not differ substantially from a fund that charges a sales load. You have to make these calculations yourself.

Some funds offer lower front-end sales loads for larger investments. The investment levels that result in sales load reductions are known as breakpoints. Funds don't have to offer breakpoints, but when they do, they have to disclose this fact in their prospectuses.

Additionally, brokers are not permitted to sell you shares in amounts just below a breakpoint. Funds vary in how they set breakpoints, and you have to seek information from each on eligibility and what the breakpoints are.

Mutual Fund Share Classes

To provide investors with choice regarding the fees and expenses they pay for services, many mutual funds issue different share classes. Regardless of class, all the shares invest in the same portfolio. Typically, class A, B, and C shares have the following characteristics:

- **Class A shares** usually have a front-end sales load but a lower 12b-1 fee and lower operating expenses. Breakpoints may lower the sales load.

- **Class B shares** usually don't have a front-end sales load but may have a back-end load and 12b-1 fee, as well as operating expenses. If you hold class B shares long enough, they may convert to a class with a lower 12b-1 fee.

- **Class C shares** may have a constant load, front-end or back-end load, as well as a 12b-1 fee and operating expenses. Usually, however, the front-end load is lower than for class A shares, or the back-end load is lower than for class B shares. On the other hand, class C shares often have higher operating expenses than A or B shares.

Mutual Fund Tax Consequences

You owe income tax on mutual fund dividends in the year you receive or reinvest them. You may also owe tax on the fund's capital gains for the year. This is separate from the personal capital gains tax you may owe when you sell shares.

You will probably owe tax on any capital gains distribution, even if the fund loses money for that year. It may be worth your while to inquire about this before investing in a fund; even if the fund is tax-exempt, capital gains distributions are still subject to tax.

By law, mutual funds have to show after-tax returns in their prospectuses, using standard formulas. You should take tax considerations into account when comparing funds.

Closed-End Funds

Although closed-end funds invest in much the same ways as mutual funds, they differ in two ways: ownership structure and ability to be traded. Closed-end funds have a fixed number of shares, the prices of which rise or fall according to supply and demand. (Mutual fund share prices rise and fall with the value of stocks owned by the fund.) Shares of closed-end funds are traded over the counter and on exchanges, unlike mutual fund shares.

Unit Investment Trusts (UITs)

A unit investment trust (UIT) is an investment company that makes a single public offering of a specific number of shares, called *units*. No further shares are issued for the lifetime of the fund. UITs usually dissolve on a fixed date, when shareholders divide up the proceeds of the fund.

Hedge Funds

These are private, lightly regulated investment pools. In many cases, they do not have many of the protective measures for investors found in mutual funds.

Like mutual funds, though, they are managed by financial advisors. Hedge funds characteristically adopt risky strategies seeking high rates of return. While mutual funds generally charge about 1.4 percent of assets, it is common for hedge funds to charge 1 to 2 percent plus 20 percent of profits.

Because these funds require relatively large investments, they are used mostly by wealthy individuals and institutional investors such as pension funds.

Exchange-Traded Funds (ETFs)

Exchange-traded funds (ETFs) resemble mutual funds but are traded like stocks. Their low costs and tax advantages make them attractive to investors.

Although their number has doubled in the past five years and they are often seen as an alternative to mutual funds, ETFs still constitute a small market. According to an Investment Company Institute count in January 2006, there are almost 8,000 American mutual funds, with a total capitalization of more than $9 trillion, while there are only 200 American ETFs, with a total capitalization of $310 billion.

I believe that the numbers of ETFs will continue to increase. They are now ranked by Morningstar, as well as by Lipper and Standard & Poor's.

The first ETF, the S&P Depository Receipts (SPDRs), appeared in 1993. Other well known ETFs include DIAMONDS (Dow Jones Industrial Average), Cubes (Nasdaq 100), MSCI EAFE Index Fund, and iShares Lehman 1-3 Year Treasury Bond Fund. Many of the ETFs available have even lower operating costs and more tax advantages than index funds.

Initially, the ETF sponsor sells shares in large blocks to brokers. Investors buy them from the brokers in much smaller quantities and trade them like stocks. Investors can't sell back ETF shares to the sponsor, as they can mutual fund shares. They sell them instead to specialists or market makers, middlemen who then swap the ETFs with the sponsor for the stocks they represent.

This in-kind payment is a nontaxable transaction, because the sponsor is not trading on the open market. The result is that ETFs are some of the most tax-efficient investments available. The low costs and low tax liabilities add up over time and can be a valuable contribution to any portfolio.

CHAPTER EIGHT

*Some Great Intangibles: IRAs,
Annuities, and Life Insurance*

Having as many different kinds of retirement plans as you can is a strong defense against economic uncertainty after retirement. The federal government certainly encourages this approach through tax laws and regulations.

However, the tax advantages associated with utilizing retirement plans should not create a big puzzle for your heirs to figure out. A financial advisor can help coordinate your retirement assets into a cohesive whole, so that there is no duplication or waste.

In times past, pensions were most retired people's sole source of income, apart from Social Security, interest on savings, and dividends from securities. Over time, inflation has reduced the purchasing power of their fixed pension dollars and left many without the assets needed to enjoy retirement to its fullest.

All the same, people are only reluctantly abandoning the "old, three-legged stool" of retirement security: employer-provided pensions, Social Security, and retirement savings. Whatever their drawbacks, pensions today have never looked more attractive—or more endangered.

According to the Center for Retirement Research at Boston College, 83 percent of workers were covered by a traditional pension in 1980, while only 41 percent were covered in 2003. In several highly publicized cases, major companies have escaped their pension responsibilities by declaring bankruptcy.

To cut costs, established profitable companies are now freezing pension benefits, which they can do with 45 days' notice for non-unionized employees. Even more widely, companies are passing responsibility for retirement to employees by changing from traditional pension plans to defined contribution plans such as 401(k)s and cash-balance plans, which are a mix of traditional and 401(k) plans. In a 401(k) plan, a company can make matching or profit-sharing contributions when profits are strong and reduce or eliminate contributions in bad years. Such a plan provides a company with more flexibility and creates a more predictable cost for the employer.

401(k)s are usually invested in mutual funds. In the best plans, employee contributions are matched dollar for dollar by the employer. 403(b)s are much the same as 401(k)s, but they're restricted to government, school, and non-profit employees. In recent years, these so-called annuities have been increasingly replaced by 401(k)s.

Another plan known as the 457 is often referred to as a *deferred compensation* plan and is established by state and local governments, tax-exempt governments, and tax-exempt employers.

Younger people in the workforce today—possibly including your heirs—tend to have low expectations about company pensions and Social Security. (If you have both, be thankful!) They foresee their retirement benefits coming mostly from funds that they control themselves. Thus, individual retirement accounts (IRAs) loom larger in their minds than they did in those of earlier generations.

In this chapter, we look very briefly at IRAs and other retirement plans. In Chapter 12, we talk about how they can be passed on to your heirs without going through probate.

In this chapter, we also look at annuities in more detail because they are often unjustifiably ignored by financial planners and writers. This chapter closes with a look at why life insurance can be as important late in life as it had been earlier.

IRAs and Other Retirement Plans

There are now a number of retirement plans to choose from. Your personal requirements can make one far more desirable than another.

The IRA and the 401(k) are the most widely used vehicles for retirement savings. The Roth versions are favored by those who want to leave their money to heirs or expect to keep adding to the IRA in retirement.

The Roth 401(k) came into use on January 1, 2006, and General Motors was the first large firm to offer them to its employees. If you want one for yourself, you may have to request it specially.

The table below briefly outlines the basics of the more commonly used retirement plans.

	401(k)	Roth 401(k)	IRA	Roth IRA
Employer Sponsored	Yes	Yes	No	No
Contributions	Before tax	After tax	Before tax	After tax
Tax paid upon redemption	Yes	No	Yes	No
Income limits	None	None	$110,000 single; $160,000 married, filing jointly	None
Maximum contribution in 2006, if 50 or older	$20,000	$20,000	$5,000	$5,000

SOURCE: *New York Times*

In mid-2006, Congress was planning to allow high-income taxpayers to convert their traditional IRAs into Roth IRAs, which would provide tax savings in later years. You can't roll retirement assets directly into a Roth IRA. You must first roll the money into a traditional IRA and then convert that to a Roth IRA, a taxable event.

Those who are self-employed can make use of SEP and SIM-PLE IRAs. These plans permit you to save more and have more flexibility to roll the accounts over. Business owners can take deductions both as an employer and employee.

However, SEP-IRAs are being replaced by 401(k)s. Anyone who is self-employed, even part time, or who owns an unincorporated business can set up a Keogh plan.

A major pitfall has emerged in recent years. Those who loyally and trustingly put all their 401(k) investments in the company they work for can have a painful outcome, as Enron, Lucent, United Airlines, and General Motors employees have learned. For your own protection, I would recommend never investing more than 10 percent of your 401(k) funds in the firm that employs you.

When you are given the choice of taking your retirement plan in a lump sum payment or in a series of payments over time, you need to dicuss the pros and cons with someone knowledgeable. Your decision may be different if you are retireing permanently or are taking a new job. Do you want the distrbution paid directly to you or to a new trustee or plan administrator? Are you better off rolling your retirement plan into an IRA in your name? What are the tax consequences of your decision? Your individual circumstances will dictate the wisest choice and professional guidance can be invaluable.

Annuities

Basically, an annuity is an investment contract between you and an insurance company in which you agree to deposit money with them. In return, they agree to pay you a predetermined interest on the sum and return it at a fixed future date.

If you withdraw your money sooner than agreed upon, you may have to pay a surrender charge. However, most contracts offer free withdrawal provisions.

In many respects, an annuity is like a bank certificate of deposit (CD), but it has these important differences:

• Annuity yields are generally higher than CD yields.

• You can avoid probate in passing annuities to your beneficiaries.

• Annuity interest is tax deferred, while CD interest is taxed annually.

• You can arrange lifetime payments from your annuity that you can never outlive.

• Annuities are not FDIC insured.

Fixed annuities should not be confused with variable annuities, which we will discuss in the next section. With fixed annuities, you are paid a predetermined interest rate. With variable annuities, your payments generally depend on how well your invested money does.

Some financial advisors and commentators dismiss annuities out of hand, mentioning the fees, lack of flexibility, and surrender charges involved. When they do this, most are directly or implicitly comparing IRAs with annuities.

Other advisors see how valuable annuities can be for retirement money unprotected by IRAs or other means. I regard annuities as a viable option you cannot afford to overlook or ignore. They come in two kinds: immediate and deferred.

Immediate Annuities
Many people who buy immediate annuities do so because they are concerned about outliving their financial resources. They pay a

lump sum to purchase single premium immediate annuities (SPIAs) in exchange for lifetime payments that begin immediately. The size of the lifetime payments depends on the amount invested and the purchaser's life expectancy.

In buying what is called a straight life or non-refund immediate annuity, you can convert a modest savings account into a steady stream of payments lasting your lifetime. However, in exchange for lifetime monthly payments, you give up the right of recovering your investment as a lump sum.

In the *Wall Street Journal* of April 5, 2006, Jonathan Clements described how a woman of 65 with $100,000 to invest tried to decide between an annuity that provided lifetime income, and high quality bonds. The annuity would have brought her an annual income of $7,336.

But, fearful that early death would cause her annuity investment to be lost, she chose bonds instead, which had been recently yielding 5.7 percent. Although the market value of the bonds could be affected if interest rates rose quickly, she was attracted by the fact that there was no charge to sell them. She intended to sell off the bonds slowly over the years for income.

She withdrew $7,336, leaving a balance of $92,664. Over the first year, that amount grew at 5.7 percent to $97,946— only a couple of thousand below her initial investment. After 10 years, at the age of 75, her bond fund was still worth more than $73,000.

By the age of 88, however, her withdrawals of $7,736 and the progressively smaller interest from her shrinking bond fund left her with a balance of only $7,000. Had she purchased an annuity, she could have looked forward to payments as long as she lived.

Today, the average American can expect to live to the age of 85. The woman in the story above ran into trouble because she lived 3 years beyond the average life expectancy—a feat that MetLife says 39 percent of Americans will accomplish. Those people can be big winners with straight life annuities.

Besides a straight life annuity, you can purchase other kinds of immediate annuities—for example, a joint and survivor annuity, which continues payments to the second person after the death of the first.

Period certain annuities are obtainable for 5, 10, 15, or 20 years. If you die before the end of the period certain, payments are made to your designated beneficiary until the end of that period. However, it's possible to outlive this kind of annuity.

Single life annuities with 5 to 25 years certain also guarantee payments to a beneficiary in the event of death.

You pay taxes only on the interest component of each payment, not on the total payment.

Deferred Annuities
A fixed tax-deferred annuity continues to earn interest and grow until you reach the age of 100. You pay no taxes if you are not taking withdrawals from the annuity contract. This greatly adds to its growth.

For example, Henry buys a $25,000 CD and a $25,000 deferred annuity, both at 6 percent interest, which amounts to $1,500 per year. Because he is in the 28 percent tax bracket, he has to pay $420 in taxes on the $1,500 interest from the CD, leaving only $1,080 to compound the next year.

Because he owes no taxes on the deferred annuity, it grows by the full $1,500. With compound interest over the years, his deferred annuity increases in total value in a spectacular way in comparison to his CD.

Henry pays taxes only on the interest withdrawn from his deferred annuity. He controls the tax years in which he makes random withdrawals. Although the annuity is part of his taxable estate, on death Henry has arranged to avoid probate in transferring it to his beneficiaries. His heirs can then choose how to withdraw the value of the annuity based on the terms of the contract.

It is advisable to discuss your options with a professional familiar with annuities and the various settlement options.

Split Annuities

A split-funded annuity is a combination of immediate and deferred annuities structured to produce immediate tax-advantaged payments for a specific time and to return the original investment at the end of that time.

In the following example of a split annuity, $100,000 is invested for 10 years at an interest rate of 5.5 percent. The $100,000 investment is split into an immediate annuity of $41,457 and a deferred annuity of $58,543. In this example, 81 percent of the income is not taxed.

Immediate Annuity: $41,457	Deferred Annuity: $58,543
Monthly income: $427.98	Year 1: $61,763
Annual income: $5,135.76	Year 2: $65,160
10-year income: $51,137.60	Year 3: $68,744
Income not taxed: 81 percent	Year 4: $72,525
	Year 5: $76,513
	Year 6: $80,722
	Year 7: $85,161
	Year 8: $89,845
	Year 9: $94,787
	Year 10: $100,000

SOURCE: *Annuity Advantage*

Fixed-Indexed Annuities

With a fixed annuity, you know exactly the amount of interest credited to your annuity contract. With a *fixed-indexed annuity*, also known as an *equity-indexed annuity*, you can benefit from a rising market by getting higher interest payments.

The interest rate paid by a fixed-indexed annuity is typically tied to an equity index, such as the S&P 500 or Russell 1000. The annuity company may also offer a bond index as a choice when setting up your annuity allocations. Whatever choice is made, using an indexed annuity allows the annuity owner to benefit from a rising market. Many companies will go even further and guarantee a minimum interest rate that will be earned regardless of the performance of the applicable index. Various formulas and procedures are used by companies to set the interest paid, and these need to be scrutinized before a purchase is made.

A fixed-indexed annuity can be a viable part of your portfolio. Because the annuity return is linked to the performance of an index, you are not directly invested in the market and therefore are not exposed to losses when the market goes down. At the same time, because you are not directly invested in the market itself, you are not going to realize the advantages of dividend reinvestments and other benefits you would enjoy if you were directly invested.

In some cases, such an annuity can be particularly useful in constructing the fixed-income portion of your portfolio. The number and types of fixed indexed annuities available in the marketplace are numerous and you should consult an advisor who understands how they can be used as tools in creating a sound financial plan. Their use always depends on your personal objectives.

Variable Annuities
In a variable annuity, you choose what to invest in, and the value of your annuity depends on the performance of your choice. Typically, you choose mutual funds that invest in stocks, bonds, money markets, or some combination of these three. You may buy the annuity with a single or series of payments, and your payments may begin immediately or at some future date.

You may select periodic payments over your lifetime. Variable annuities have a death benefit. If you die before your annuity payments begin, your beneficiary receives an amount usually at least equal to your total purchase payments.

Taxes are deferred in variable annuities in much the same way as they are in fixed deferred annuities. According to the SEC, however, variable annuities (as well as fixed annuities) confer no added tax advantages to money already in IRAs or employer-sponsored 401(k) plans.

I believe that variable annuities will provide a viable source of income for many soon to be retired baby boomers. There are many different options and income benefits that can be tailored to meet your personal objectives.

The important thing is to find an advisor who understands annuities and who can explain to you how to accomplish your goals. A competent advisor can set up a variable or other kind of annuity as part of your retirement plan.

Life Insurance Now?

It's easy to see why someone starting a family in a newly acquired home needs life insurance. However, many people on the verge of retirement see little reason for having any. It's not always clear to them that they can use life insurance to provide for their families in much the same way as people just starting out.

In the event of the policy owner's death, the insurance company typically sends a check in just a few weeks. The payment is tax-free and avoids probate, as long as the estate is not named as the beneficiary of the policy. The money can be used to meet a family's immediate financial needs, such as providing money for funeral costs and daily living expenses.

The proceeds can also permit a period of grief that is free of economic pressure. Additionally, it can pay off a mortgage, pay estate taxes, and function as an emergency fund. As well as being an investment and asset in itself, life insurance is an effective means of protecting your other investments and assets.

How much life insurance do you need? You may need enough to see your family through six to nine months of probate, unless you have provided for them by other means, such as a trust. Many people use five to ten times their annual incomes as a rule of thumb. A financial advisor can provide you with a far more realistic sum, reflecting your individual situation.

You can expect that your family's living expenses will be at least 75 percent of what they are presently. Although life insurance settlements usually involve a single lump sum payment, some companies offer guaranteed monthly settlement options.

Who should be the owner of the life insurance? If it is in your name, the proceeds become part of your estate and thus may be subject to the estate tax. A sizable policy can raise the value of your estate beyond the federal tax exemption.

If the policy is in your spouse's name, the problem of policy size and federal tax laws still must be considered. Many people who own large life insurance policies utilize an irrevocable trust as part of their estate plan. We discuss trusts in Chapters 14 and 15. Such trusts are complex and need to be set up by a professional.

In most states, no estate tax is due if the life insurance policy was transferred to an irrevocable trust more than three years before the death of the policy owner, or if it was initially purchased by the trust. In many states, creditors have no access to such trusts.

If your minor children are the beneficiaries, a trust permits a trustee named by you rather than a court-appointed guardian to supervise the distribution of benefits. You can gift enough money each year to the trustee (you can designate one of your adult children, if you wish) to pay the premium on the policy.

If you have a large IRA and will not need it for living expenses, you can use your required minimum distribution to pay the annual premium on a large life insurance policy. For example, in this way, you might turn a $100,000 IRA into a $500,000 benefit for your heirs.

What kind of life insurance do you need? There are two basic kinds—term and permanent. We now look at each.

Term Life Insurance

Term life insurance provides for the payment of a specific sum to the beneficiaries of the policy owner, if that person dies within a specific period. If the policy owner survives that period, the policy becomes invalid and no payment is made.

Premiums for term are lower than for permanent insurance, making the former attractive to people of limited resources who need a lot of insurance at a particular stage in their life. This also appeals to companies covering the life of a key employee.

Benefits are generally tax-free. A term policy can usually be converted to a permanent policy without a physical examination or answering medical questions.

Term insurance premiums may be level or may increase with age. The policy itself has no cash value and provides no tax-deferral advantages. Once the term expires, the policy is worthless.

Permanent Life Insurance

As its name implies, permanent life insurance provides a payment on the death of the policy owner without a time limitation. Although premiums for permanent insurance are higher than for term insurance, they are fixed and thus over time may prove to be less expensive.

After a certain time, a permanent insurance policy accumulates a cash value that you can borrow against. However, if the loan and unpaid interest exceed the cash value, your policy may be canceled. The cash value growth is usually tax deferred, which means that you can borrow money on the policy without having to report it as taxable income. You can generally borrow up to the amount you have already paid in premiums.

Many policy owners use these loans for their children's college tuitions and for retirement projects. Such loans, of course, reduce the benefit payable to beneficiaries after your death. If you cancel a permanent insurance policy, its accumulated cash value is yours, less some surrender charges and taxes.

Permanent insurance comes in two basic kinds: *whole life* and *universal life*. Whole life insurance is generally a straightforward arrangement in which, for a specified benefit on death, fixed premiums are paid throughout life by the policy owner. It tends to have the highest premiums, but also the most guarantees.

Universal life insurance has a more flexible policy in which you can vary the timing and amount of premiums; you can also change the death benefit. Premiums can be credited to an interest-paying policy account from which mortality charges are deducted.

The choice of policies is almost as wide and at times as confusing as that of mortgages. Professional advice increases the likelihood that you will make the selection most suited to your needs.

The Whole Picture

What assets to hold, what to buy, and what to get rid of may be your opening questions when planning with a financial advisor. He or she may see potential in some assets that you hold in low regard or alternatively may not be as optimistic about some assets as you are.

You may be pleasantly surprised when you review your assets and find yourself in a more prosperous position than you realized. When moving, people often find they own more furniture than they believed. When planning their estates, they are apt to discover that they are worth more than they knew.

In the next chapter, we discuss what to look for in a financial advisor, and how to find one.

CHAPTER NINE

Finding a Financial Advisor

After reviewing the different kinds of assets you can hold in your search to ensure your continuing quality of life in retirement, you may decide that you can benefit from some professional advice.

You almost certainly can use counseling on which asset mix best reduces your risk, yet provides an opportunity for growth and income. And you very probably require at least some input on monitoring and rebalancing your portfolio. Few people in the investing world try to go it alone—for very good reasons.

Financial professionals share information with one another more readily than people do in other industries. It's not that they have hearts of gold; they share new information with their colleagues because they need the same in return. What goes around comes around.

Most private investors, on the other hand, do not receive the ongoing education that such information confers, so they usually can't compete against professionals who know more. Through their market contacts, financial advisors can help to better serve and guide their clients throughout the retirement years.

Even long-term investors, who are not looking to make a killing on price twitches in the marketplace, need a constant stream of information to educate themselves about market changes. To make the right long-term decisions, you need the relevant information.

"If only I'd known that," I've heard people say, "I wouldn't have done it." Well, too bad for them. In the marketplace, it's up to people to keep themselves informed. That has always been the way.

You are not timing the market or selecting the securities—you are allocating assets among the available classes to obtain the best return at an acceptable risk level. I actually tell my clients (whether or not they believe me is another story) that I do not know any more than they do about where the market is heading.

But you do not need to. I aim to provide my clients with the method, tools, and guidance to help them achieve their objectives, which is the information that they need. As an investment professional, I need to stay informed about new developments and innovations in finance. I do this, but I do not feel it necessary to worry every day about the state of the markets.

A financial advisor can also help simply by being a sounding board for your ideas or wishes. He or she is going to follow your investment strategy more closely than you would, without authorization to follow whims or hunches. An experienced financial advisor's objectivity, discipline, and lack of emotional decision-making can really pay off over time.

In addition, an experienced advisor is more likely to be successful in asset allocation and portfolio rebalancing. Although, like in any profession, you can't assume that all or even most financial advisors have knowledge and skills in these areas.

What to Look For in an Advisor

There should be a minimum of three meetings between investor and advisor. In the first, you get to know one another. We will discuss the second and third meetings in the next section.

The following concerns are very important in the first meeting:

* **Be forthcoming.** The more the advisor knows about your aims and concerns, the better he or she can take them into account when structuring an investment proposal.

* **Personal aspects.** When you first meet a prospective advisor, measure him or her on a personal level. Think of your possible relationship as a partnership, which it actually would be in a fee-based arrangement. On an instinctual level, do you want a working partnership with this person? Can you communicate easily? Do you feel comfortable with him or her? These personal issues are important, because if you don't click as people, you may not work well as partners.

* **Trustworthiness.** The advisor should strike you as a stable, responsible individual in whom you can place your trust. Although this is hard to describe, most of us are competent judges of a person's honesty and stability. We can sense these qualities even if we can't say exactly how we do it. Your need for trust in your financial advisor can't be overemphasized. You must feel convinced that this person will put your economic well being before everything else.

* **Registered Investment Advisor.** Selecting who to talk to can be confusing, but one question I would ask the advisor you are interviewing is whether he or she is a registered investment advisor—which would mean that he or she has a legal fiduciary responsibility to give you the best possible counseling. Registered investment advisors have to put

your interests first and disclose problems and conflicts. They must provide clients with a Form ADV, which shows the services they offer, how they are compensated, their business connections, and any SEC penalties. These advisors are held to a higher legal standard than stockbrokers and most other financial professionals. They are required by law to act in your best interests.

- **An advisor who knows about asset allocation and modern portfolio theory.** Your prospective advisor maybe caring and hardworking, but if he or she does not under stand or cannot fully explain the benefits of asset allocation and diversification, I would encourage you to keep interviewing. If the advisor's talk is all about hot stocks and big winners, it's time for you to move on and look elsewhere.

- **Absentee owner.** If this is what you want to be, let the advisor know. But also let the advisor know that although you won't be looking over his or her shoulder, you expect monthly statements and quarterly reports that you will examine closely—even if you do so in the shade of a palm tree.

- **Fee-based compensation.** Stockbrokers, some financial advisors, and other financial professionals are paid by the number of transactions they complete. They earn little or nothing when an investor sits tight. So, it's natural that their clients wonder at times whether their advice to trade is based simply on a desire for income-generating activity. This conflict does not arise with a fee-based financial advisor, who generally charges an annual fee of 0.75 to 2.00 percent of the value of your portfolio's assets, often times regardless of the amount of trading. To increase their income from you, they have to increase the value of your portfolio—a win/win situation. On the other hand, if you have a bad investment year, their income drops proportioately. This is why I earlier described a fee-based relationship with an advisor as a partnership. You go up or down together.

Meetings With the Advisor

Your first meeting with a prospective advisor will determine if there should even be a second. Clearly, if the first meeting does not create a sense of confidence in your mind about this person, you should not go any further.

To be fair to advisors, first meetings often prove unsatisfactory because investors don't quite know what they want. Some advisors are patient with ditherers, but others regard this as a waste of time and make no effort, feeling they can't assist people who don't know their own minds.

If, in a first meeting, you find an investment advisor who you like and can communicate with easily, who knows about asset allocation and modern portfolio theory and who seems to care about your financial well being, arrange a second meeting to go over your assets, investment goals, and risk tolerance.

Bring a folder to the second meeting containing copies of documents and anything else that may be useful, and leave this folder with the advisor. Make sure he or she understands two things: what you want from your investments and how much risk you are willing to assume. As we have discussed, people in retirement usually wisely settle for a less than spectacular return in exchange for a lowered level of risk.

Provide a phone number (and email address if possible) where you can be reached. Encourage the advisor to contact you at any time with questions, big or small. Don't bother insisting on formality with someone to whom you are handing over the secrets of your economic life.

In the third meeting, the advisor should make investment proposals and have detailed explanations for each. It's very important that you should be able to understand these proposals. Don't be blinded by technical terms. If something can't be explained in plain language and can't be understood by people with life experience, such as yourself, it's probably not for you. Be forceful.

Anything arcane or complicated is probably also risky to someone who doesn't understand it. This doesn't mean that you need to understand the economic theory and trading details—only that the investment concept should make sense to you.

After you've had time to consider the advisor's investment proposals, you may need a fourth meeting for further questions or explanations. But, you may not. In any case, the advisor should remain open to your further inquiries and comments, as well as provide you with quarterly updates on your portfolio status.

Conclusion

Selecting a financial advisor can be one of the most important decisions you make during your lifetime. After all, this choice has the potential to affect you today and well into the future.

It is my hope that you use the information contained in Part I of this book as a roadmap of what to look for and which questions to ask. I have always believed that education is the key to almost anything you do in life. By becoming informed of the options available to you when selecting a financial advisor, you will provide yourself with the necessary information to make an informed and intelligent decision.

Armed with this information, you can chart a course toward a life free from the day-to-day worries of how your investments are being handled with the knowledge that you have a trusted professional minding the keys to the store.

Liberty Asset Management

I feel, at this point, it is appropriate to provide you with a little background information regarding our firm. The basic investment philosophy of Liberty Asset Management is simple: you need to invest passively for the highest return at the risk level at which you are comfortable.

The best practical way to reduce risk in your portfolio is through diversification by means of asset allocation. To put together such a portfolio, most investors need assistance from financial advisors. Indeed, advisors themselves need assistance from other professionals in the market. In the financial world, no man (or woman) is an island.

Even while competing with one another, all professionals have the need to be part of the information gathering process and other networks. At Liberty Asset Management, we are no exception.

Liberty Asset Management was founded with the objective of bringing a truly passive investment strategy to our client base. Most of our clients have been with traditional brokers, investing in the traditional, active way. Experience has shown many this is typically an uphill battle.

When they realize that they have been attempting to do the impossible (that is, consistently "pick a winner" or time the market), they see the appeal of the more rational approach offered by modern portfolio theory and the efficient market hypothesis.

As a lawyer and registered investment advisor, I have what I would call a double fiduciary responsibility to put my clients' economic well being before everything else. My ethical responsibilities can and do weigh heavily on me. This, of course, comes with the territory. For me to sleep at night, I must feel that I have done everything possible to ensure my clients have a successful investment experience.

PART II

ESTATE PLANNING AND YOUR BENEFICIARIES

Chapter Ten

Planning Your Estate

People are apt to put off estate planning until the proverbial "rainy day," regarding it as a less than pleasant activity. However, it can be seen in a much more positive light, as a way to provide for your family and to have your wishes carried out.

It requires a great deal of effort for most of us to accrue assets—and since we can't take them with us, we can at least control their distribution after we have gone. Maintaining such control helps to ensure that the people or causes you intend to benefit actually receive your gifts. All it takes is planning with a little foresight—and usually, some professional advice.

There are numerous other benefits to estate planning. On the practical side, you can save your family fees and bureaucratic delays through intelligent planning. You can gain an emotional benefit by bringing your family together and explaining your plans, thus creating greater intimacy and harmony between your future benefactors and you.

You need to be open to suggestions from family members. For example, you may be unaware of some of the jealousies and conflicts that exist among them. While you don't want to pander to such personality issues, you also don't want to inflame them unintentionally. In addition, any of your earlier actions that might have seemed unfair to some family members can be remedied when everyone is together.

Your estate is likely to consist of real estate, tangible personal property (furniture, vehicles, and so on), and intangible personal property (securities, bank accounts, benefits, and so on). A good first step is to make an inventory of your assets. What should be done with them?

Pay special attention to ongoing businesses and the decisions that may need to be made. The executor of your will may not have the knowledge or ability to make them. Additionally, his or her judgment may be adversely affected by the stress of trying to guess what you would have done in the circumstances. Simple guidelines from you can indicate possible solutions that may not be obvious to someone without your understanding of the business.

Your inventory should state clearly all your income sources and regular expenses. You cannot assume that your family members will want to play detective and work out the complexities of your estate.

Minimizing taxes and preserving the value of what has been accumulated is often a primary aim of those who plan their estates. A carefully drafted estate plan can help to ensure this goal is realized and that your beneficiaries are receiving as much as possible. In many situations, the savings in taxes alone can more than cover the cost of retaining a professional to help you plan for the future.

The fewer issues you leave unresolved, the less confusion there will be in the future. As you did in life, you can help and even directly influence the lives of those closest to you.

To sum up, when you plan your estate, you can do the following things:

- Control what happens to your assets.
- Provide for your loved ones.
- Provide for other individuals.
- Contribute to worthy causes.
- Avoid family conflict over division of assets.
- Speed up the legal process of passing on your assets to your beneficiaries.
- Minimize the costs of the process.
- Minimize the tax liability.
- Look out for yourself by providing for your final years.
- Make a living will.
- Arrange to sell or continue your business.
- Contribute further to your current peace of mind.

Estate Planning Choices

At speaking engagements, I often tell people that they basically have four choices to make about estate planning:

1. Do nothing.
2. Let your spouse inherit everything (joint tenancy).
3. Make a will.
4. Use a trust.

As a lawyer and financial advisor, I frequently find that many people I meet for the first time are utilizing one of the first three methods to plan their estate. In my opinion, the fourth option—a revocable trust—is often a more advantageous solution for those interested in preparing a plan that benefits them both today and in the future.

In this chapter, we will look at the pros and cons for each of the first two options: doing nothing and joint tenancy. In Chapter 11, we look at what's involved in making a will and how probate affects your heirs. In Chapters 12-14, we consider ways in which you can pass assets on to heirs that do not involve going through probate, including by way of a revocable trust.

Do Nothing

If you don't plan your estate, you need to realize that the state you reside in will do it for you. State law determines who gets your property under the laws of intestacy. Furthermore, your estate is likely to go through probate.

Most states have laws that require probate of assets that exceed a certain value, and you should determine your states rules when deciding what to do (or what not to do). We will look more closely at probate and why you might want to avoid the process in the next chapter.

If you own real estate in more than one state, your properties will be disposed of according to the laws of the states in which they are located. Again, this might mean that your assets will not be distributed as you wish.

If you don't care what happens to your assets after you are gone, you are an unusual person. Most whose assets are distributed by the state had not intended for it to happen—they simply kept putting off estate planning and were caught unprepared.

If you die intestate (without a will), the state seeks out your surviving relatives. Some states give everything to the surviving spouse, with the children receiving nothing. We discuss this in the next section in the context of jointly owned assets (joint tenancy).

Other states give shares to the spouse, children, and parents. For inheritance purposes, most states recognize ties by blood, marriage, and adoption, but exclude unmarried life partners and stepchildren.

Before deciding that doing nothing is a good option, check how the laws of your state will affect your family. In Illinois, for example, if you are married and have children, your spouse would receive half your assets and your children the other half. If your children are under age, however, their property may be administered by a court-appointed guardian, which may result in conflict and expense.

If you have no family, relatives, or deserving causes, doing nothing may be a reasonable option. The state will probably "inherit" your assets. In most other cases, the worst choice of the three would be to do nothing. For this very reason, I encourage most people to prepare a Last Will and Testament, at the minimum.

Joint Tenancy: Till Death Do Us Part

Married couples are often tempted to avoid estate planning and let events take their course. This approach has a strong appeal. The surviving spouse gets everything and avoids probate—and meanwhile, no one has to bother making a will.

This method of planning, if you want to call it that, is frequently attempted by holding assets as joint tenants with right of survivorship. Upon the death of one joint tenant, by operation of law, the ownership of their assets passes to the survivor. No will…No lengthy legal process…No costs… This choice sounds ideal—until you consider the problems that are likely to occur.

If you have children or particular bequests you want to make, the possible problems of joint tenancy are obvious. Other problems your beneficiaries are likely to encounter may not be so easily anticipated. We now look at important problems that often occur.

Joint Tenancy Problems

It is extremely common for a married couple to hold assets as joint tenants. However, joint tenancy can involve joint ownership for life partners, friends, parents and children, and other relationships.

All too frequently, many take joint tenancy for granted, without considering or perhaps even being aware of alternative forms of joint ownership. They are often surprised by the serious problems that lurk in this seemingly simple and straightforward process; the following are some of the most frequently encountered:

- Probate only temporarily avoided
- Wishes not followed

- Financial risk
- Loss of asset control
- Tax exemption loss
- Capital gains tax in community property states
- Gift tax

Probate Only Temporarily Avoided

Simply put, probate consists of court validation of a will, appointment of an executor or representative (titles may vary from state to state but the job is essentially the same), and distribution of the estate assets. Although frequently it is not required upon the death of one tenant in joint tenancy, it often *is* required upon the death of the second. Thus, probate is only temporarily avoided by holding assets in joint tenancy.

Wishes Not Followed

With joint tenancy, you may effectively disinherit your children; the most likely to suffer are your children from a prior marriage. You also leave special bequests up to the discretion of your spouse.

If your spouse remarries after your death and predeceases the new spouse in another joint tenancy, that person will be the one to dispose of your hard-earned assets. At that point, your children or other loved ones may be deprived of what you wanted them to have. You presently have the ability to prevent these or other unpleasant outcomes from occurring.

Financial Risk

When you hold assets in joint tenancy with someone, regardless of whether it is your spouse, you are considered to hold, for the sake of simplicity, a half share. You can lose your half share if your joint tenant owes back taxes or bad debts or declares bankruptcy. Court-awarded damages against your joint tenant or a divorce can also result in loss. At the very least, you leave yourself vulnerable to financial misfortune through joint tenancy.

Loss of Asset Control

You likely take for granted that you have control over what you own. But in joint tenancy, you surrender total control and may have to obtain your joint tenant's consent before selling an asset or using it as collateral.

Your joint tenant's spouse, when it is not you, may have wishes opposed to yours. Your joint tenant may prove unpredictable for emotional reasons. His or her actions may threaten or deplete the value of assets, and his or her legal complications or illness may cause the jointly owned assets to be frozen.

Tax Exemption Loss

A federal exemption permits married couples to pass up to $4 million of assets free of an estate tax, and individuals up to $2 million. Without any advanced, post-death, estate planning techniques, in joint tenancy, there is no exemption used upon the death of the first tenant, and the second tenant receives only a $2 million exemption.

When your estate is large enough for taxes to become an issue, you are effectively wasting one person's exemption with the use of joint tenancy. With proper estate planning, the entire $4 million exemption can be preserved.

Capital Gains Tax in Community Property States

When you sell an asset at a profit, you generally have to pay a federal capital gains tax on the profit. The price you originally paid for the asset is called your cost basis.

A federal tax law provision, known as a *step up in basis*, permits your beneficiary to set the cost basis of an inherited asset at its current value. Thus, if you bought the asset for $100,000 and it is worth $200,000 at the time of your death, your beneficiary can set its cost basis at $200,000.

If he or she later sells the asset, capital gains taxes are due only on the amount that exceeds the new cost basis or date of death value. That said, as of this writing, the tax laws relating to stepped-up basis are set to change in 2010 if no further action is taken by Congress.

In the end, you should consult with a knowledgeable advisor to determine the tax consequences of your planning decisions.

If you live in or own real estate in a community property state, however, on your death, your spouse receives the step up in basis exemption for only half an asset held in *joint tenancy,* rather than held as community property or owned outright by you. For the asset mentioned above, bought for $100,000 and worth $200,000 at your death, your spouse owes capital gains tax on $50,000 on its sale for $200,000.

In states other than the nine with community property laws, your spouse owes nothing in capital gains tax. With proper estate planning, your spouse can also owe nothing in a community property state.

Community Property States
Arizona
California
Idaho
Louisiana
Nevada
New Mexico
Texas
Washington
Wisconsin

Gift Tax

Customarily, people don't view joint ownership as being restricted to married couples. In relation to taxes, however, the government generally does.

Parents often confer joint ownership of houses, cars, land, investments, and bank accounts on their grown children. Grandparents may do the same for a grandchild or young nephew or niece. Friends make investments together informally. Many are outraged when the IRS claims that these conveyances are gifts and the donor is found to be liable for a gift tax.

As of the publication date of this book, you can give up to $12,000 to as many individuals as you wish without the gift tax applying. The lifetime ceiling (applicable exclusion) for gifts to individuals is $1 million.

What does the IRS view as a gift that you might not see that way in a traditional sense? Adding someone's name who is not your spouse to a title of ownership often qualifies. With jointly owned bank accounts, the gift tax may apply only when the added person withdraws funds for personal use. The person who made the so-called gift is liable for gift tax rather than the person who withdrew the funds.

If a parent adds a son's or daughter's name to the title of their home as a co-owner, the IRS may find the parent responsible for a gift tax on half the value of the house. Adding a name in itself may or may not trigger the gift tax, but it generally should be reported on a gift tax return. Failure to report the transaction may result in penalties and interest far larger than the gift tax itself.

It goes without saying that estate planning can be complicated and professional advice can be indispensable here.

Alternatives to Joint Tenancy

Being aware of the downside is more than half the battle. The following are alternatives to joint tenancy.

To use a legal term, *tenancy by the entirety* treats the parties as a unit that is much less affected by the individual circumstances of the joint tenants. However, it does not apply in all states. Tenancy by the entirety is a form of co-ownership that applies only to a husband and wife, viewing them as one person for the purpose of owning property.

All agreements must be signed by both. Each owns the whole property and cannot divide it into parts and neither can separately sell, mortgage, lease, or cause it to be subject to a lien. Each has the right to sole ownership when the other dies. It is therefore necessary that any document relating to property held in a tenancy by the entirety be signed by both husband and wife.

In some states that recognize tenancy by the entirety, unless the deed specifically states otherwise, real property conveyed to a husband and wife is held in this form. In states that do not recognize it, a deed requesting tenancy by the entirety may result in the property being held as *tenants in common* or *joint tenants with right of survivorship.*

In some states, if a husband and wife divorce, their tenancy by the entirety automatically converts into a tenancy in common, with each ex-spouse owning a half interest in the property. In a few states it converts to joint tenancy with rights of survivorship. Consult with your attorney to determine the laws in your state regarding such matters.

Tenancy in common is a way in which two or more people can own property together. Upon death, each can bequeath his or her share to his or her beneficiaries and exclude the heirs of their spouse or co-owners, which is not possible with joint tenancy.

In some states, tenancy in common is presumed to exist between spouses or co-owners unless otherwise specified in writing. Tenancy in common is more often used by business partners than married couples, although there is no reason why the latter should not make use of it.

Other options exist, such as *payable-on-death* (POD) and (TOD) asset designations. Frequently, bankers and brokers tell their clients to title their accounts POD or TOD, saying that when they do this, the accounts will avoid probate and all their beneficiaries will have to do is present ID and a death certificate to claim the assets.

While this is accurate, the bank POD or brokerage TOD agreements often do not adequately provide for what should happen if one of the beneficiaries predeceases the account owner. Does the agreement state that the deceased beneficiary's children (if any) are to receive the deceased beneficiary's share (per stirpes) or does the account go to the surviving beneficiaries?

Moreover, what if the deceased beneficiary's share is going to his or her children and those children are minors? In this case, the account assets may have to be distributed to a court-appointed guardian in a custodial account.

This form of ownership is not a substitute for an estate plan. Why run the risk that your wishes will not be followed, when it is so easy to prepare a plan? I will have more to say on POD and TOD designations in Chapter 12.

Although a POD or TOD option may have a place within the context of your plan, neither can compete with thoughtful estate planning by an experienced advisor, who may recommend such alternatives as a revocable living trust (Chapter 14).

In the next chapter, we deal with the third choice about estate planning: make a will.

CHAPTER ELEVEN

Should You Make a Will?

A will is a document providing for the distribution of estate assets after the death of the person who signs it. The person who creates the will is known as the testator. It is usually signed in the presence of at least two witnesses (see Essentials of a Valid Will this chapter).

A simple will describes the straightforward distribution of assets of an uncomplicated estate. A *last will and testament* may also provide for the creation of a trust—known as a *testamentary trust*. Such a will sets up one or more trusts into which some of your estate assets will go after your death. A perceived disadvantage of such an arrangement is that the estate assets may go through probate prior to being distributed to the trustee of the trust(s).

A *Pour-Over-Will* leaves some or all of your assets to an already existing trust or trusts. Again, we will look at trusts in Chapters 12 through 14.

A husband and wife or any two people can make a joint will, though this is not what I would recommend. Such a will may prevent the survivor from disposing of assets, fail to allow for changed circumstances, be extremely difficult (if not impossible) to revoke, and have estate tax consequences. A so-called *living will* is not a will in this chapter's meaning of the word. Rather than disposing of assets, it instructs doctors and hospitals regarding the use of life support in the event you are unable to do so.

Making a will is one way to request that your wishes are followed after your death. However, probate is one of the biggest disadvantages to consider when using a will to pass on your property. Probate is the often lengthy legal process of putting the will into effect. We will look at further aspects of this later in the chapter.

Final Instructions Letter

Your assets may be tied up for a year or more in probate. Therefore, you need to make arrangements for any immediate expenses, such as funeral costs, bills due, and other debts that will survive you. (By the way, you may use your will to forgive debts owed to you by others.)

To do this, you can leave a letter with your final instructions where it will be quickly found by your loved ones. Sending copies to the executor of the will and your lawyer further ensures the letter's rapid discovery. Some people use these letters to limit funeral expenses, donate organs, request cremation, ask for charitable donations instead of flowers, or make other specific requests. But survivors are not legally bound by such a letter, as they are by a will.

It's also a good idea to use this letter to provide important information that people already possess but may have forgotten about or misplaced. Provide your Social Security number and that of your spouse, as well as any existing insurance policy numbers. The names and phone numbers of your lawyer and the executor of the will should be included.

Mention the location of important documents such as birth, marriage, and divorce certificates, as well as business, financial, pension, and insurance records. State where safe-deposit boxes are located and how to go about accessing the contents. Some people indicate what they want mentioned in their obituaries.

Life insurance can take care of immediate expenses after your death. A joint bank account can provide your spouse with an immediate income. Adding your spouse's name in advance to at least some of your credit cards and bank accounts can greatly ease cash flow problems immediately after your death.

Essentials of a Valid Will

The laws regulating wills and probate vary from state to state. What is acceptable in one state may not be in another. If care is not taken when initially establishing your will your heirs may find themselves with a big mess on their hands.

The American Bar Association selected the following seven essentials as those that make a will acceptable in most states:

- *You must be of legal age.* Eighteen is the legal age in most states, although you can be younger in some and need to be older in others.

- *You must be of sound mind.* This means that you must understand what a will is, be aware of the assets you are bequeath ing, and know who is getting them. People often challenge a will on grounds of testamentary capacity, meaning the testator was not of sound mind at the time the will was executed. But it is not easy to succeed in this, because the standard of proof is high. A person being absentminded or forgetful is not enough.

- *Your last word.* You must say that this is your will or at least that this is how you wish your property to be disposed of after your death.

- *Put it in writing.* By tradition, a will is a document that has been signed and witnessed, although some states accept unwitnessed oral or handwritten (holographic) wills. Electronic wills are accepted in Nevada.

- *Sign it properly.* If the testator's signature does not conform to the requirements of state law, the will may be invalid. Signing must be voluntary. If illiteracy or a physical handicap prevents the testator from signing, one of the witnesses or a lawyer can sign in that person's place.

- *Witnessed properly.* Most states require that at least two adult witnesses sign a will. They must understand what they are witnessing and be competent to testify in court. Most states also require that the witnesses be disinterested—that is, they received nothing in the will themselves. If a witness proves to be a beneficiary, this may provide grounds to challenge and perhaps invalidate part or all of the will.

- *Executed properly.* A properly executed will ends with a statement that this is the testator's will and gives the place and date of signing. The will should also state that the testator signed it before witnesses, who then each signed it in the presence of the testator and the other witnesses. Self-proving affidavits are accepted by most states, so that witnesses do not have to testify in court that they witnessed the signing of the document.

What to Put in Your Will

Keeping your will straightforward and highly specific may help shorten its time in probate. For anything other than an outright transfer of ownership, it may be best to use a trust.

The language used should clearly express your intention. For example, a precatory gift is one that you wish to make—you don't command it.

The requests that you put in your will need to carefully identify assets and beneficiaries. For example, you may have more than one landscape painting and more than one niece named Jennifer. Being specific about who gets what helps avoid the misunderstandings and squabbles over inherited assets that are typical of many families.

Executor's Role

You can choose one or more executors to administer your estate. To lessen delay and probate court proceedings, you can have your lawyer draw up your will so that the executor has power to resolve issues and solve problems. You can even direct that the probate court should have minimal involvement. Moreover, giving the executor flexibility can be very time saving, particularly when you own a business or unanticipated circumstances arise.

Residuary Clause

Having assets not disposed of in your will can cause big delays. Rather than being concerned about whether you have thought of everything, put a residuary clause in your will—it disposes of property you have not mentioned.

You bequeath the assets in your residuary estate to someone. In the event a named beneficiary predeceases you, the bequest to the deceased beneficiary lapses. In most states, an anti-lapse law provides for the distribution of the bequest and may result in the deceased beneficiary's heirs receiving your bequest.

Where such a law is not in force, your bequest may be distributed with the residue of your estate. Again, laws vary from state to state and you should consult with your attorney to determine the applicable rules for your situation.

Tangible Personal Property Memorandum (TPPM)

This memorandum or direction usually covers the distribution of personal items such as jewelry, furniture, and art. States vary as to how legally binding they regard TPPMs and the disposition of your tangible personal property may be determined by the terms of your will. Check with your attorney to determine how best to handle personal property.

Where to Keep Your Will

Sign only one copy and keep your signed will in a fireproof safe at home, safe-deposit box or in your lawyer's office. Some probate courts provide will storage, but this may involve public disclosure of the contents. Because safe-deposit boxes are often sealed on the deaths of their holders, it can be weeks or even months before a signed will that is stored in one is read.

To help with this problem, many states have enacted statutes that provide access to a safe-deposit box for the purpose of retrieving a will or burial documents. However, a will, if found, must usually be delivered to the Clerk of the Circuit Court in the county which the lessee resided prior to his or her death.

For this reason, don't get too ingenious about hiding your will. If it can't be found, you might as well not have bothered making it. Keep any number of unsigned copies of the will for easy reference, but to avoid possible confusion, only one signed version should exist. You may wish to make a new will in the future and it may be hard to track down all the signed copies of your old will if more than one exists.

Changing or Revoking Your Will

Over the years, you will probably find it necessary to make alterations to your will, to meet changing circumstances. Some people review their wills once a year, often on or around their birthdays.

Crossing out words and writing in changes or additions may or may not be legally accepted. It's much safer to use a new page to present your changes or additions formally in what is called a *codicil*. The formalities required for the valid execution of a Last Will and Testament must be present when making a codicil.

A major life change is the usual cause of revoking a will. The best way to do so is to make a new will that mentions and revokes the old one. Some lawyers recommend destroying the old one in the presence of witnesses, while others say it is better to keep it as support for the new will's legitimacy.

Probate

Probate is the court-supervised process of asset ownership transfer and debt payment after someone's death. All 50 states have enacted laws governing most aspects of the probate process.

The size of your estate will play a part in determining the procedure involved in passing on your assets. For example, in Illinois, probate occurs when assets held in an estate exceed $100,000. When estate assets amount to less than that amount, a *small estate affidavit* may be used to transfer ownership, except in cases where real property is being passed on.

As noted above, laws vary from state to state and you should consult your attorney to determine the rules in your state.

Probate's positive aspect is that it enables an orderly and lawful transition. Its negative aspect is the amount of time (and money) it takes to do so. Although the duration of probate has been shortened in many states during recent years, heirs can generally expect a wait of six months to a year before they receive what is due to them. If there is a legal challenge or some complexity, the wait can be much longer.

With probate, a family finds that it has surrendered control to the court and must follow an often inflexible and sometimes costly legal process. In most states, the procedure is more or less as follows.

Probate begins with a petition submitted to the court to open the estate. In a court hearing six weeks to two months later, if there is a will, it is validated and an executor is confirmed. Challenges, complexities, and disputes are reviewed. Assets are frozen while an inventory is made.

In cases of special need, particularly for young children, the handicapped, or the seriously ill, the court may grant a family allowance in which creditors are given a date by which all claims must be filed. Taxes are paid.

To close the estate, the executor usually has to file forms with the court to show that all claims against the estate have been settled, all disputes have been resolved, and all taxes have been paid. Before distributing the assets to the beneficiaries, the court deducts legal expenses—although many states permit an early partial distribution of assets to help ease financial hardship. Assets may lose value through neglect during a lengthy probate period.

Should You Avoid Probate?

Many people would avoid probate if only the alternatives were easy. For a couple of decades, *How to Avoid Probate* was a paperback bestseller. When this book was popular, probate was well worth avoiding because of its excessive delays.

More recently, many states have simplified and speeded up the legal process. Because probate law varies from state to state probably more than any other kind of law, it's worth checking the ones that apply in the state in which you reside. A lawyer who practices in this area can counsel you on what probate-avoidance techniques are worth your while.

You don't necessarily avoid probate by either making or not making a will. Keep in mind that your will is generally not effective until it goes through probate, and if it is contested or not validated for some reason, your beneficiaries can expect the probate process to be lengthy and costly. If you don't make a will and joint tenancy does not apply, your state will likely supply a will and probate for you.

In the next few chapters, we will look at how you can pass on assets without a will and probate. Trusts are one way to do this—but if a trust is mentioned in a will, it does not become effective until after the will has been probated.

Giving your assets to your children or others avoids probate, but keep in mind the annual exclusion and laws pertaining to gifting. Additionally, you may not want to give away assets that you may need in the future, and don't expect to continue controlling the assets after you have given them away.

Your children may lose or dispose of the assets, which can cause bad feelings in the family if you make your opinion known. Giving a family member power of attorney to distribute your assets can work during incapacity, but becomes invalid upon death.

If you have a straightforward will and an uncomplicated estate, probate may be a desirable route for you to take. Although your heirs may have to wait six months or more for your gifts, you can most likely be assured that they will receive them. Probate has the force of law behind it.

On the other hand, if you are leaving behind an ongoing business or unresolved issues, or if you intend to favor some family members and exclude others, you need professional advice on the best course of action. Don't accept some one-size-fits-all advice from the Internet or a book. You need an attorney to identify and take advantage of the possibilities offered by your individual situation.

Cutting Probate Costs

With the expectation that at least part of your estate will pass through probate, here are some cost-cutting factors recommended by the American Bar Association.

• Seek professional advice.

• Keep your will up to date and properly prepared, with clearly and simply stated bequests.

• Make an inventory of your assets.

• If you have children by more than one spouse and list them all as beneficiaries, avoid ambiguous or easily misunderstood phrasing.

• Does the size of your estate qualify it for any simplified probate procedures?

• Instruct your executor to follow any simplified probate procedures that your state may allow.

• If you own real estate in other states besides the one in which you reside, instruct your executor to contact a probate attorney in those states.

• Instruct your executor on how to handle any ongoing business.

• Discuss your wishes with your family and other beneficiaries.

Your Most Immediate Concern

People often procrastinate about making a will or bequeathing their assets in other ways. Although that is very understandable, you can make the biggest financial mistake of your life by not planning.

You probably already have a clear idea of who you want to get what. You may have given the matter some thought. But unless you take timely action, things may not turn out as you intend. Instead of leaving grateful beneficiaries behind to share warm memories of you, your inaction may initiate family feuds—sometimes over trifling objects and amounts.

Indeed, some malevolent individuals deliberately leave their affairs in disorder with the intention of stirring up family discord. It is sad when someone kind and well meaning leaves a legacy of disharmony instead of a well-planned estate and grateful heirs.

Act now. You can influence the ways in which your loved ones remember you.

CHAPTER TWELVE

Using a Trust to Bequeath Assets

As a way of bequeathing assets, a *last will and testament* has the desirability of being a formal legal process for transferring assets upon death and the undesirability of probate.

As you read in the last chapter, probate is a court process that can be time consuming, frustrating and often costly. Fortunately, there are ways of passing on assets that can have a will's legal strength without the drawbacks frequently associated with the probate process.

These ways may be used in place of a will or in addition to one. In any event, you will best accomplish your goals by discussing your intentions with a knowledgeable estate planning attorney.

I have previously recommended a trust as one of the most advantageous ways to pass on assets to beneficiaries. There are other ways to avoid the delay and expense of probate, and we now look very briefly at them before examining what is involved when using a trust. We have already discussed some of them.

Ways to Avoid Probate

We have seen that life insurance is one way to provide almost immediate money for your loved ones. Life insurance proceeds can help them meet the financial demands they are faced with, such as household expenses, funeral costs, and tax liabilities.

Joint tenancy helps you avoid probate when the first spouse passes away. However, since the estate of the surviving joint tenant is often subject to probate upon his or her death, it's just delayed rather than avoided.

An IRA with your spouse or another survivor named as the beneficiary becomes the immediate property of that person when you die, without going through probate. The many options associated with an inherited IRA, however, warrant consultation with an advisor to take full advantage of all the available tax benefits.

In some states, real property can be left to someone through a beneficiary deed. Generally speaking, the owner of the property may still sell, encumber, and deal with this property without restrictions or limitations.

Furthermore, you can typically revoke this deed at any time and it does not become effective until your death. Again, however, as we have seen with other simplified probate avoidance strategies, there are drawbacks, and this technique should be discussed with a competent estate planning attorney prior to being implemented as part of a plan.

Also, in many states, the law may provide for a transfer-on-death (TOD) designation that accomplishes the same thing as a beneficiary deed. TOD and payable-on-death (POD) designations are used to avoid probate in many states for bank accounts, savings bonds, private company stock, and brokerage accounts. These designations can be revoked at any time. A POD account has been called a Totten trust in some states.

Gifting is another method for avoiding probate. A gift of valuable property—for example, a home, stock, or even cash—removes the asset from an estate and the probate process. However, there are legal and tax considerations when making gifts and remember, you are giving up control of your property.

Again, it is a matter of education. You must understand the implications of the strategy you are implementing in order to make an intelligent decision, and professional advice is recommended.

Although each of these ways of avoiding probate has advantages—often, low cost and simplicity—none compares to the advantages of a revocable living trust.

What Is a Revocable Living Trust?

A trust is a legal relationship in which you, the grantor (or donor, trustor, or settlor), have a trustee hold property for a beneficiary. The trustee is usually a person, but may be a trust company or bank in some cases.

The beneficiary can be almost anyone or anything you choose. The property held in trust can be almost anything. In fact, as long as state laws are observed, trusts are generally not strictly defined. In a trust, you no longer officially own the property—and this is where the advantages mostly reside.

The trustee holds legal title to the trust property and from a legal viewpoint is its owner. The beneficiary holds an equitable or beneficial interest, giving him or her rights as specified in the trust.

A *living trust* (also known as an "Inter Vivos Trust" or "Grantor Trust" is one that permits you to add or remove assets during your lifetime and for which you yourself can be grantor, trustee, and beneficiary. A revocable living trust is one that you can revoke at any time.

This is a good option to have, but there are tax considerations involved. For tax purposes, your ability to revoke the trust qualifies you as its owner. You have to count income from a revocable trust on your personal income tax return.

In contrast, an irrevocable trust generally cannot be revoked. Furthermore, trust income is reported by the trustee on a separate tax return.

Types of Trusts

There are many different kinds of trusts. In preparing this chapter, I began by listing some of the types, but abandoned this as too confusing and at times misleading.

A trust can be made very flexible and can be drafted to meet your needs by a competent estate planning attorney—and this is what is important to understand. Your requirements dictate the kind of trust that may be best for you. You need not adapt your needs to fit a trust. Trusts are flexible enough to fit anyone's needs.

Is a Trust Worth Your While?

Trust fund kids, it is sometimes said, never have to wake up to the economic realities of life, and most of us probably feel that this is not necessarily a good thing. No doubt, some people with great inherited wealth have few or no money worries, but most who benefit from trusts lead everyday lives. Their trust income increases the quality of their lives, but usually does not erase all economic realities and concerns. In other words, trusts are not only for the very wealthy.

I am often asked who does not need a trust. My answer is simple: if you don't care what happens or you have little or no assets, you probably do not need one. But almost everyone else with something to pass on (especially those who own real estate) can benefit from using a trust.

You should always pay a professional to set up the trust. In exchange for this, you may receive tax planning benefits, eliminate the need for court supervision in case of disability, protect your beneficiaries from creditors, or ensure some personally desired fund distribution or protection.

Obviously, you need sufficient funds to make the effort and cost of setting up a trust worthwhile, but the clarity of your wishes may be more important than the size of your estate. A trust, like a will, is a way to have your wishes carried out after you have gone. Unlike a will, however, a properly drafted and funded trust minimizes or eliminates probate court delays.

Structuring a trust to meet your individual requirements is of paramount importance. Do not choose from some previously prepared menu. You need to set up a trust that uniquely fits your needs.

The best way to go about doing so is to find an advisor with qualifications, experience, and pride in his or her work—plus patience and honesty. Finding such an estate planning attorney can yield more significant results than researching trust types on your own.

Tax Considerations
Beneficiaries who inherit below the present federal estate-tax exempt amount of $2 million per person do not have to pay federal estate taxes. However, they do have to pay federal income tax on the income they get from trusts.

When they collect the trust principal, they do not have to pay tax, except in states with an inheritance tax or in the case where there is a capital gain. The table below contains the federal estate tax exemption amounts in effect as of publication.

Current Federal Estate Tax Exemption:	
Year	**Applicable Exclusion Amount**
2006	$2,000,000
2007	$2,000,000
2008	$2,000,000
2009	$3,500,000
2010	Estate Tax Repealed
2011	$1,000,000

Taxes owed on income generated by the trust are paid by the trustee, from the trust principal. However, if the trust income is distributed to the beneficiary, that person is responsible for paying the income taxes.

The kinds of investments chosen by the trustee can affect the amount of taxes a trust owes. When the trustee and beneficiary are the same person, tax advantages may be lost. As mentioned earlier, this can also happen when a grantor retains control over a trust, as in a revocable trust.

People are often unpleasantly surprised to discover that there may be state as well as federal estate taxes. While Congress is presently considering further legislation, the *federal* estate tax on estates above the $2 million personal tax exemption is presently 46 percent. This rate drops to 45 percent in 2007, drops to zero in 2010, and climbs to 55 percent in 2011. Further changes are likely, and even abolition of federal estate taxes is possible.

But you cannot assume that *state* estate taxes follow the federal pattern. For example, while the federal personal exemption is planned to rise to $3.5 million in 2009, the Illinois state personal exemption is scheduled to remain at $2 million. In Wisconsin, Minnesota, Ohio, and 10 other states, the state personal exemption is less than the federal $2 million.

In New York, it is presently $1 million. Thus, someone in New York who owes no federal estate taxes on an unsheltered $2 million estate may owe $99,600 in state estate taxes, according to a tax lawyer quoted by the *New York Times*. You almost certainly need advice from a professional on state estate taxes if you live in a state that has them.

If you have a substantial estate, trusts can help you reduce or even eliminate estate taxes. In your own lifetime, you can use a trust to give tax-free gifts each year to your children, grandchildren, and others, thereby reducing your taxable estate. A knowledgeable advisor can structure a trust that makes use of the marital deduction and avoids what is known as the generation-skipping tax.

Living Trust Strong Points

Every strategy has its pros and cons, and living trusts are no exception. But the pros outweigh the cons more for living trusts than they do for most strategies. Here is a list of some of the advantages:

- **Avoids probate.** The assets in a living trust pass directly to the beneficiaries. However, assets not titled in the trust name may be subject to probate.

- **More flexibility than a will.** You can provide instructions to a trustee that you cannot to the executor of a will. For example, you can have the trustee distribute assets over time to beneficiaries (say, your grandchildren) or manage assets over time on behalf of some beneficiaries.

- **Avoids state law variability.** In some states, you cannot appoint a child who lives out of state the executor of your will. But, you can appoint him or her the trustee of your liv-ing trust. If you own property in more than one state, one living trust can provide for the probate-free distribution of all the property, in contrast to multiple probate filings in different jurisdictions.

- **No complications.** A revocable living trust is very flexible to manage because nothing really changes for you. You can add or withdraw assets from your trust at any time without the assistance of an attorney. You still hold property in your own Social Security number and generally, you are still filing your income taxes as you have always done in the past.

- **Protects privacy.** Unlike a will, no public record is required of a living trust. In some states, however, a public record must exist if a living trust contains certain assets such as real estate, securities, or a safe-deposit box. Your advisor may find a way around this through a nominee trust or partnership if you desire.

- **Management.** You can appoint a trustee to manage your affairs if you are no longer able to or no longer wish to do it yourself.

Living Trust Drawbacks

As previously mentioned, the disadvantages of living trusts are minimal in comparison to their advantages. Below are some examples of the perceived drawbacks of a living trust:

- **Higher cost.** You generally pay more to set up a living trust than make a will, although the eventual cost of probate with a will should be taken into account.

- **Creditors and Claimants.** When using a will, in most instances, creditors and claimants will be barred from making claims against your estate after a period of time. A properly drafted trust can supply the trustee with the power to address those cases where creditors may be an issue.

- **Supervision.** A will going through probate is overseen by the courts. A trustee does not answer to the courts (unless a dispute arises) but to the beneficiaries. Remember, the main part of the word trustee is trust. You must implicitly trust the trustee you have named to handle your estate.

- **Maintenance and updating needs.** You need to make sure you are keeping assets in the name of the trust, to ensure that your wishes are followed and probate is avoided. This is as simple as telling the banker you want to hold your CD in your trust name rather than as joint tenants.

- **Third Parties.** Banks, brokers and insurance companies want proof of your trust's existence. We always provide clients with a certificate of trust evidencing the creation of the trust agreement and a summary of the important terms.

Unrealistic Expectations

Some people are so enthusiastic about revocable living trusts that they credit them with powers and advantages they do not have. Here are some of the mostly widely encountered false beliefs about having a revocable living trust:

- **People believe that you do not need a will if you have a living trust.** You usually do, in order to bequeath property that you failed to hold in the trust name, and in some cases to deal with other matters.

- **People believe a revocable living trust helps reduce income tax.** As we discussed earlier, the IRS regards the ability to revoke a trust as continued ownership of the assets held in the trust name. If you are the grantor and ben eficiary, you are responsible for paying the taxes.

- **People believe a living trust protects assets from creditors.** An irrevocable living trust may, but not a revocable one. Again, a properly drafted revocable trust will provide your trustee with the powers necessary to deal with creditor issues.

- **People believe it is not possible to challenge a living trust.** While it is generally harder to challenge a living trust than it is a will, it can be done—and usually for the same reasons.

- **People believe that there are never delays with living trusts.** Generally, there are not, but the accounts of an ongoing business or debts that need to be settled by the trustee may cause a delay. Such delays are only rarely as long as those of probate.

As you have read, you will be well served by taking the time to educate yourself regarding the use of a revocable trust as part of your estate plan. We look next at what is required in establishing one and the importance of maintaining a properly funded trust.

CHAPTER THIRTEEN

Setting Up and Funding a Revocable Living Trust

It goes without saying that you need the help of an attorney when setting up a revocable living trust. Finding an experienced advisor can help you avoid the many possible pitfalls. Once a mistake has been made or a precaution overlooked, it can be troublesome to correct.

Although the legalese and terminology can be complicated, listen carefully to your advisor, because the decisions to be made center on your personal wishes.

Revocable or irrevocable? In cases where tax planning is of the highest importance, or if you have more advanced planning objectives as are often found with small business owners, it may be worth your while to sacrifice your power to make changes and use an irrevocable trust. You might limit the number of assets transferred to it and beneficiaries named in it, hoping that this simplification will make a later desire for change less likely.

In almost all other cases—particularly if you have a residence, perhaps a vacation home, and other commonly held assets—the option of making changes and retaining control should probably not be given up. That is, choose a revocable trust.

Couples must decide for themselves whether to set up one or two trusts. While two are frequently used for large estates and second marriages, the choice revolves around tax planning considerations and your plan objectives. An experienced attorney can help guide you. Remember, your requirements dictate the type of plan that is best for you.

Many couples choose to share assets in a joint trust. When a spouse dies, the survivor may take control of the assets without any conditions or limitations. Again, the results depend on the choices you make when speaking with your advisor and setting up your estate plan.

Sub-Trusts

For tax and legal purposes, a trust may be discussed as if it consists of several parts; there may even be more than one trust involved. Yet, in most cases during the grantor's life, it remains a single trust.

The division of a trust into sub-trusts, frequently referred to as AB trusts or ABC trusts, is a common cause of confusion. For a joint trust created by a couple, as long as both spouses are alive, the sub-trusts essentially remain inactive. Upon the death of the first spouse, depending on the terms, the sub-trusts may be activated and assets funded into each. We will discuss funding a trust later in the chapter.

Sub-trust A is commonly referred to as the "marital share" or "marital trust" and will hold assets as determined by the terms of the trust. I have found it easy for some to remember this distinction by referring to Sub-trust A as the "above ground" trust.

Upon the death of the first spouse, it is common for estates requiring little or no tax or legal planning to have sub-trust A hold all of the assets that were in the joint trust. In such cases, very little needs to be done when the first spouse dies, as the surviving spouse (trustee) retains complete control over the entire trust estate.

Sub-trust A may be viewed as merely an extension of the original joint trust established by the parties. It remains revocable for the life of the surviving spouse as long as he or she is competent.

Sub-trust B, commonly referred to as a "family trust" or "credit-shelter trust," holds assets determined by the terms of the trust. You can refer to Sub-trust B as the "below ground" trust. It is frequently used when an estate exceeds the federal estate tax exemption amount, or when there are more complicated distribution issues being addressed within the trust.

As discussed in an earlier chapter, the current exemption for the year 2006 is $2 million per person. Assets held in the estate upon the death of the first spouse that exceed $2 million can be funded into sub-trust B so as to utilize fully the decedent's federal estate tax exemption.

Sub-trust B is an irrevocable trust and its terms will dictate how the property is to be handled. You can provide your spouse with rights to income and principal, as long as you follow certain guidelines.

Sub-trust C is commonly referred to as a Q-TIP (qualified terminal interest property) trust. It is frequently used when you want your spouse to have access to the income from the assets held in the sub-trust, but you do not want him or her to have the rights to principal. Your goal may be to provide an income source for your spouse but to preserve the assets for your heirs.

Sub-trust C is also irrevocable and must be drafted following certain guidelines. Additional considerations must be given when your spouse is a non-citizen. In such cases, a trust created for the benefit of the non-citizen spouse must generally meet the requirements of a QDOT trust or qualified domestic trust. One such requirment is that the trustee or at least one of the co-trustees be a U.S. citizen.

I have referred to sub-trusts so far in the context of planning done by a husband and wife. For those who are single or widowed, the use of sub-trusts is not applicable as relating to the tax considerations explained above.

As mentioned earlier, each individual has the ability to pass on a certain amount of assets without incurring a federal estate tax. Those who are single or widowed have one exemption and the need for such sub-trusts is simply not present. If you fall within this category and your estate is large enough to warrant tax planning, you should consult your advisor to determine the best course of action.

For those with estates under the exemption amount, a trust is, in my opinion, the best way to avoid probate and pass property on to your loved ones.

In addition to the sub-trusts described above, you may also create other sub-trusts for purposes not relating to tax planning. You may be in a second marriage and want to provide for your spouse while preserving assets for your children from your prior marriage. You may have a child or loved one with special needs that warrants the creation of a *supplemental needs trust.*

You may want to create a sub-trust for a child who has problems handling money. You may have a child with an unstable marriage and you do not want to see his or her inheritance going to the spouse. You may simply want to create a sub-trust as a way to pass property on to your grandchildren or great-grandchildren.

Your options are unlimited. Trusts are very flexible planning tools that allow you to pass property on to your beneficiaries without the delay and expense of probate. However, as can be seen from the brief summary above of how trusts can be structured, the legal and tax planning considerations dictate that you seek the advice of a competent estate planning attorney. Remember, the devil is in the details.

The Role of Trustee

When you establish a revocable trust during your lifetime, you begin by placing some or all of your assets in the hands of a trustee, for the benefit of your beneficiaries. You can be the trustee; your spouse can be co-trustee or suceed you as trustee in the event you become incapacitated or pass away and you can have one or more of your children as successor trustees. Alternatively, you can appoint a trusted and responsible friend or professional as trustee or even a trust company.

Although setting up a trust normally involves a bit more work than preparing a simple will, particularly if your estate plan is complicated, being trustee of a properly structured trust generally involves little work.

A trustee can only do what he or she is authorized to do as specified by the terms of the trust. If the granted powers are too restrictive, a trustee may not be able to do what is clearly required. Since you cannot foresee all the eventualities when drawing up a trust, it is often better to err on the side of caution by giving the trustee broader powers, rather than too few.

A wise trustee pays close attention to what the trust advisor says. A good advisor will recommend keeping accounts by the ledger method, maintaining separate checking accounts for any sub-trusts and following the prudent person rule of conservative investing.

An advisor can explain a beneficiary's rights—including the rights to income, right to the principal to maintain the same standard of living, and a frivolous right to $5,000 or 5 percent of the asset value, as an example.

Furthermore, being trustee is not a life sentence. You can surrender the position at any time by writing a simple letter of resignation. As indicated above, you have named a successor trustee to take your place in the event of your resignation, incapacity or death.

Ancillary Documents

In setting up a living trust, your advisor will, in most cases, suggest drawing up what are called *ancillary documents*. While a properly drawn up trust makes your wishes clear in unambiguous terms and needs no additional explanatory documents, these can provide protection for you, your estate, and your beneficiaries.

They generally consist of the following:

- Pour-Over-Will (Last Will and Testament)
- Durable Power of Attorney for Property
- Durable Power of Attorney for Healthcare
- Nomination of Conservator or Guardian
- Nomination of Guardianship for Minor or Incapacitated Children
- Living Will

Having these ancillary documents drawn up according to your wishes ensures that your plans will be enacted, even if you are unable to oversee them yourself. However, remember to store the ancillary documents with the trust or at least in a place where they will be found without search or delay.

Let's briefly look at each of these documents.

Pour-Over-Will (Last Will and Testament)

A pour-over-will is simply a new will that you create when establishing a living trust. It is used to revoke any old will you may have created and to handle the distribution of any assets that may not be held in the name of your trust when you pass away.

The pour-over-will normally names the trust as the beneficiary of any assets not held in the trust name. The presence of assets not held in the trust and covered by the terms of the pour-over-will may result in probate taking place. Therefore, as you will learn below, it is important to maintain a properly funded trust.

Durable Power of Attorney for Property

Conferring power of attorney on someone means giving them the right to make financial decisions on your behalf in the event of your being unable to do so yourself. The powers granted to your agent are terminated upon death.

Conferring on someone durable power of attorney for property makes that person what is known as an *agent or attorney-in-fact*. Deep trust and understanding should obviously exist between that person and you. In the event of your incapacity, the attorney-in-fact must adhere to the powers granted him or her in the document. The powers granted may be broad or restrictive. But, you generally do not want to make the powers too restrictive so as to prevent your agent from carrying out your wishes and being able to effectively manage your affairs.

You may grant your agent the right to add assets to your revocable trust. If you had not already done so, this person could even create a living trust for you. However, the rules vary by state and it is important to discuss your objectives with your attorney.

Durable Power of Attorney for Healthcare

Many couples rely on each other to make any necessary healthcare decisions when the time comes. This understanding assumes that one survives and retains the capacity to make such decisions.

When both are seriously injured in a car crash, for example, the weakness of such an arrangement is exposed. Your spouse and you each need a separate, durable power of attorney for healthcare. Ideally, these documents would nominate alternate or successor agents to make healthcare decisions for each of you.

Parents can make medical decisions for their minor children, but when your children or grandchildren turn 18, each needs his or her own document.

Nomination of Conservator/Guardian

A nomination of conservator/guardian names the person responsible for your physical well being in the event of your incompetence. This is distinct from a durable power of attorney for healthcare, which confers the power to make healthcare decisions on your behalf.

The person designated by this nomination actually checks on how you are being cared for and physically treated. Naturally, you should choose someone with the ability and character to carry out such duties.

In Illinois, for example, you can provide for the nomination of a guardian within the terms of your durable power of attorney for healthcare. Again, you should discuss this with your attorney in determining the best course of action for ensuring that your wishes are followed.

Guardianship of Minor or Handicapped Children

A single or remarried parent with legal custody of minor or handicapped children is likely to be concerned about what happens to them should he or she die or become incapacitated. A document nominating a guardian for such children can specify who you would like to be responsible for them.

However, in most states, the nominated person must petition the court to be formally appointed, and the court must believe that such an appointment is in the "best interests" of the child. This legal process can be simple or complicated, depending on the circumstances, and it frequently results in the parties involved hiring an attorney to handle the process.

Living Will

As I mentioned in Chapter 11, a living will is not really a will in the legal sense of a last will and testament. The document may be made out with the general form and terminology of a will, or it may be in the form of a healthcare proxy or right-to-die clause. Your attorney can recommend the form favored in the state in which you reside.

Most people use a living will to request the liberal administration of painkillers and to stipulate that life be allowed to follow its normal course—that is to say, they do not want their life artificially prolonged through the use of technology. Many seek advice on this beforehand at their church or temple.

While a desire to avoid physical suffering motivates people to make a living will, so too does the wish not to burden their children or grandchildren with such a disturbing choice.

Funding Your Living Trust

You need to review an inventory of your assets with your advisor to decide what to put in your living trust and what to leave out. The process of transferring assets into the name of your trust is formally referred to as "funding" the trust.

To transfer an asset into the trust, you need to change its title or registration from your name to that of the trust. If you are the trustee, you must always observe which hat you are wearing— that of *Your Name* or that of *Your Name, Trustee*—and sign accordingly.

To transfer your home and other real estate from your name into your trust, you need to have a new deed prepared for each property, transferring title to the name of the trust. The deed should then be recorded with the county recorder's office. Doing so provides you (as trustee) with a clear title for the future. You can sell the property, take out a mortgage or home equity loan, and otherwise deal with the property as you always have, only now you are acting as a trustee.

Moreover, this transfer should not affect the status of your home mortgage. But, to avoid possible confusion, you may want to notify your lender when transferring your residence into your trust. This is especially important if you own additional real estate and are carrying a mortgage on the property. A good estate planning attorney will generally oversee this process.

You may run into bureaucratic resistance at some credit unions or small financial institutions about transferring your account from your name into that of your trust. In such cases, you usually have the alternative of giving your account a payable-on-death (POD) designation, with your trust named as the beneficiary.

However, trusts have become such frequently used estate planning tools that most financial institutions will be willing to help you complete the transfer process.

You should also transfer title to non-retirement account investments such as your stocks, brokerage accounts, and mutual funds. In most cases, your advisor or attorney will be more than happy to assist with this.

With securities, if you run into resistance, you can give them a transfer-on-death (TOD) designation, with the trust as the beneficiary. Again, the common usage of trusts as estate planning tools rarely requires that you handle your securities in this manner.

If you reinvest dividends, your broker probably maintains a dividend reinvestment account in your name, which may at times contain relatively substantial amounts. Do not forget to transfer this account into the name of your trust.

Unless you fully understand the tax consequences, you should not name your trust as the beneficiary of an IRA. Generally, retirement plans, as well as life insurance and annuities, are passed on by naming a beneficiary rather than placing them in a trust. These are the kind of individual issues that an experienced advisor can address.

To sum it up, you have spent a lifetime accumulating assets, and you will be well served in the future to take the appropriate steps to oversee the management and distribution of your estate. A trust can be one of the greatest gifts you can give your family (and yourself), but it is important that you understand the legal and tax consequences of setting up a trust.

A competent advisor who is there for you today and in the future will provide you with the peace of mind that your wishes will be followed and your goals realized.

CHAPTER FOURTEEN

Starting a Dynasty Trust

The use of a trust to preserve wealth and provide for the future financial well-being of loved ones has long been a primary objective of those creating an estate plan. The *rule against perpetuities*, which varies from state to state and is intended to limit the length of trusts, generally dictates that a trust cannot last longer than the life of someone alive when the trust was created, plus 21 years. As an example, if you used your infant grandson as what is known as the measuring life and made him and his children beneficiaries, the trust probably would not last much more than a hundred years.

In response to a demand from people with substantial estates who want longer or even perpetual trusts, almost half of the states have eliminated the rule against perpetuities and allowed for the establishment of what are commonly referred to by the legal profession as *dynasty trusts*.

I prefer, in speaking with clients, to refer to such a trust as a "gift trust" or "family wealth trust." The reason for this is that most people do not feel that they are creating a dynasty and do not respond to this term in relation to planning for their future. For the purposes of our discussion in this chapter, however, I will refer to it as a dynasty trust, as this is what most attorneys have come to call it.

147

You can call it whatever you like, but the end result is the same: **the creator of the trust has a made a conscious decision to plan for the future and create a legacy.**

In states not enforcing the rule against perpetuities, a dynasty trust can last for hundreds of years or even forever. When properly structured, the money in it can pass through many generations without being subject to estate taxes, allowing the amount to compound to an amazingly large sum of money.

Dynasty trusts can remain in effect as long as local law permits. Generally speaking, most states will fall into one of three categories regarding the duration of a dynasty trust:

- States that adhere to the common law rule against perpetuities, which, as noted above, requires that the trust must end 21 years after the named life in being (probably the youngest beneficiary named).

- States that have adopted the Uniform Statutory Rule Against Perpetuities, under which the trust must end as provided for in the rule against perpetuities or, alternatively, after 90 years.

- States that have abolished the rule against perpetuities which permit a dynasty trust to last for an unlimited period of time.

As with most other estate planning techniques, the laws regulating the use of dynasty trusts can change at any time. You should consult with a competent estate planning attorney to determine the applicable laws in your state and how best to accomplish your objectives.

In Chapter 2, we looked at how money can compound over time. The following is another example.

Richard has three grandchildren, the oldest 10 years old and the youngest 3. He has provided a $100,000 trust for them that will become available when the oldest turns 65.

At that time, each grandchild will be entitled to a one-third share of the trust fund, which by then will total over $6.3 million, assuming an annual growth rate of 8 percent. Each would receive more than $2 million from Richard's original total investment of $100,000.

Age	$100,000 Investment at 8 percent Compounded Annually
10 (oldest)	$100,000
19	$199,900
28	$399,601
37	$798,806
46	$1,596,817
55	$3,192,044
65	$6,380,912

Estate and gift taxes are levied every time assets change hands from one generation to the next. A dynasty trust avoids these taxes by outlasting the family members and providing for future generations.

There is no tax saving for you when you create a dynasty trust. You are generally utilizing your federal estate exemption and the tax savings are realized upon the death of your descendants. The assets accumulate over the period of time specified and remain free from federal estate and gift taxes as long as the trust remains in existence.

The savings on estate taxes can be enormous. Considering that estate tax rates climb as high as 46 percent and that the tax is applied to each generation upon the transfer of the property, up to 70 percent of the estate can be saved through three generations.

For example, if the estate tax rate was 46 percent and you had a trust fund of $1, it would be reduced to 54 cents prior to your children ever receiving a penny. Assume further that your children's estate tax rate is also 46 percent; your grandchildren would only receive approximately 30 cents.

Therefore, because of estate taxes, to pass on even $300,000 to your grandchildren, you would have to start with close to $1 million.

In contrast, a dynasty trust of $1.00 is not consumed by estate taxes and keeps growing for your heirs. In fact, at a modest 6 percent annual rate of return, $1.00 would turn into $339.30 if your dynasty trust lasts for 100 years—not an impossible accomplishment.

The combination of compound interest and freedom from estate taxes can make the use of a dynasty trust a valuable wealth-building tool for those interested in creating a legacy. Although most people cannot start one with millions of dollars, many can with $100,000. That, earning 6 percent compounded annually and in existence for about a hundred years, can grow to more than $30 million.

Another way to look at this: $100,000 in today's dollars would have been approximately $5,000 in 1906, if you assume an annual inflation rate of about 3 percent. That amount invested in a trust in 1906 would have grown to over $1,600,000, assuming a 6 percent interest rate compounded annually.

This shows the amazing benefit of compounding. I give this example to dispel the thought at $5,000 dollars wouldn't buy a loaf of bread in 100 years.

Setting Up a Dynasty Trust

A dynasty trust may be created for a short term, but the trust's tax-saving impact is greater the longer it is in existence.

It is common to name the grantor's children as the primary beneficiaries of the dynasty trust. After the last child dies, the grandchildren or great-grandchildren can become the primary beneficiaries and the trust continues on. Remember, your requirements or wishes dictate the kind of trust that may be best for you.

As with a revocable trust, the dynasty trust has a trustee in charge of managing the assets and distributing income and principle according to its terms. You determine the amount of discretion the trustee has in making such distributions when you establish the trust.

As stated above, you have choices in determining the level of access a beneficiary has in obtaining funds from the trust. In cases where the beneficiaries are not financially responsible, provisions restricting access to the funds may be incorporated into the document.

"Spendthrift clauses" can be used to limit access to trust assets and can prove valuable in many situations. You can prevent creditors of a beneficiary from attacking trust assets to satisfy the payment of a debt. You can also prevent a divorcing spouse of a beneficiary from putting forth a claim to trust assets during a divorce proceeding.

Spendthrift clauses need to be drafted by an experienced attorney who understands the grantor's situation. For some, the spendthrift clause in a dynasty trust is more important than the tax savings.

From a tax-planning perspective, it is critical that no beneficiary be given an interest in or power over the trust that is too broad; this can subject the trust assets to gift taxes when distributions are made from the trust or to estate taxes on the beneficiary's death.

A dynasty trust can be set up on an incentive basis; discretionary distributions can depend on a beneficiary's making reasonable efforts to support himself or herself and his or her family. The "incentive clauses" in a trust may encourage a beneficiary to become a productive member of society and not to become overly dependent on the trust for his or her support.

A dynasty trust can be created during your lifetime, or a portion of your estate can be used to fund the trust upon death. Creating one during your lifetime allows you to leverage your $1 million GSTT (generation skipping transfer tax) exemption. Currently, each individual is given a GSTT exemption in the amount of $1 million.

Moreover, the dynasty trust shelters not only the value of the assets transferred inside it, but also any appreciation of those assets.

Funding Your Dynasty Trust

A dynasty trust should be funded with only certain types of assets. The IRS can tax the income from these trusts at very steep rates, with the top rate coming close to 40 percent.

Furthermore, the top marginal tax rate for such trusts is reached when income exceeds approximately $10,000. As a result, the assets placed inside the dynasty trust should be tax-efficient. Tax-efficient mutual funds, tax-free municipal bonds, and cash-rich life insurance are generally suitable choices.

Many grantors choose an irrevocable insurance trust in conjunction with a dynasty trust. The irrevocable insurance trust is funded with insurance on the life of the grantor. When he or she passes away, the proceeds of the policy pay any estate taxes on other assets in the estate and the dynasty trust is funded with the assets that would have been consumed by estate taxes.

Additionally, life insurance provides an immediate death benefit and is easily handled when administering an estate. Using the dynasty trust along with an irrevocable life insurance trust can provide significant peace of mind.

Three Issues

In starting a dynasty trust, you are faced with three main issues. The first is whether, considering the cost involved, it makes financial sense for you to set up such a fund. You need to estimate the amount of money that can be saved and passed on to future generations by the trust. The cost to you will be an investment in the big picture.

Second, you need to find an appropriate trustee. As well as being reliable and capable of administrative duties, the person should know and empathize with you and your family situation.

The third issue is finding an experienced advisor to set up a dynasty trust and oversee management of the assets. A wise decision would be to choose someone who is experienced in the field of preparing such trusts and has an understanding of the appropriate legal, tax, and financial considerations involved.

You may not be able to predict what happens in the future, but you can provide those you care most about with financial security. All that is required is a little forethought and motivation, and the guidance of a trusted professional. As we have all been told, "Most people don't plan to fail, they fail to plan."

CHAPTER FIFTEEN

Talking to Family Members

We all want our children or beneficiaries to have a painless and non-confrontational experience when dealing with our bequests. I often tell clients that very few people say to me, "My children argue all the time, can't seem to get along with one another, and are sure to dispute over what I have chosen to do." In fact, most say just the opposite.

Only when the voice of reason is gone do the children start to argue. Usually other parties have a role in this, often a significant other. For example, someone's wife may insist, "You're not going to let your sister take all that stuff your mom left in the house...."

A well-drawn estate plan provides few opportunities for troublemaking. It may be that you have not said much to your family about money or financial matters because you yourself did not think a lot about estate planning until it came time for you to retire. If you do not explain the circumstances, your sudden introduction of the subject may alarm your family. You may need to stress that this is long-term planning—and definitely not frantic arrangements in the final weeks of your life.

Those of us with grown children working for others may wonder what provisions they are making for the future. And how are they, in turn, teaching their children—your grandchildren—to manage money?

If you are retiring from an ongoing family business, you almost certainly have had to consider the future roles of family members inside and outside that business. There is also the need for you to be open to new ideas that your children or grandchildren may have heard about. In this chapter, we briefly discuss these issues.

Are Your Offspring Providing for the Future?

A consultant said recently that his firm was receiving a surprisingly high number of queries from retirees about teaching their grown children about money and finances. Those retiring often felt they did not want their children to repeat the mistakes they had made in financial planning. Many believed their children were managing their 401(k) plans poorly.

Hewitt Associates, an employee benefits consulting firm in Lincolnshire, Illinois, recently issued data on how different generations are managing their employer-sponsored retirement plans. The percentages of those eligible to participate in a tax-deferred 401(k) who actually do so are as follows:

Generation	Age Range	Eligible 401(k) Participants
Baby Boomers	42-59	72%
Generation X	26-41	63%
Generation Y	18-25	31%

According to Hewitt Associates, the youngest workers (Generation Y) who invest in 401(k)s can expect to replace *all* their pre-retirement incomes upon retirement. Those who do not participate can expect to replace only 43 percent of their pre-retirement incomes.

The consulting firm was struck by the conservative investment strategy of most young workers. The majority maintained a
60/40 ratio between stocks and bonds, which reflects a risk level
often considered appropriate for those in their 60s. Being this
risk-averse at 18 through 25, you can only wonder what they will
be like at later ages.

No doubt, multiple factors contribute to their high level of
caution. Lack of financial knowledge may be one cause of their
lack of confidence.

Are you willing to talk to your grown children about money
and financial management? Apparently, many parents are, but
their children often avoid doing so because it makes them seem
too eager to benefit from their parents' deaths.

Requesting your children's input on some problem that concerns you more than them is one way of opening up a discussion.
Additionally, the topic of providing for grandchildren is generally a low-stress way of talking about your estate planning and
your children's current level of financial responsibility.

Talking to Younger Family Members
How do you talk to your grandchildren about finances without having them roll their eyes? *Don't lecture.* This is the advice
of Holly Isdale, head of wealth advisory at Lehman Brothers in
New York. She suggests telling family stories to make your
points.

"By adopting storytelling as a vehicle, you can teach children the values, decision-making and ethics that are important
to the family," she told the *Wall Street Journal*. "Stories are how
values and lessons are passed down the generations."

You also need to be aware of messages implicit in your children's raising of your grandchildren. Needless to say, it makes
for smoother sailing when you don't openly criticize their child-
drearing approaches, even when strongly tempted to do so.

One valid source of disagreement occurs when parents say their children can spend money they earn themselves in any way they please. "It's their money," they may say. "They can do what they like with it." Both they and you know the kids will spend everything and save nothing.

A few teenagers with jobs save for college, but the vast majority spend everything they earn on clothes, electronics, and going out at night, which they may do three or four times a week. According to the market research firm Teenage Research Unlimited, of Northbrook, Illinois, American teenagers spent $107 billion of their own money in 2005.

William Doherty, a University of Minnesota professor of family social science, told the *Wall Street Journal* that parents need to negotiate an arrangement with their kids on how much they spend and how much they save. "But teenagers hate micromanagement," he warned. "It drives them to secrecy, lies and rebellion."

Parents also need to be realistic about short-term saving in relation to a teenager's wages. College fees and reliable cars are beyond what can be attained, but car insurance is within reach.

Even when young people openly disagree with parents or grandparents, they often follow the advice they are given. Money is only one of the issues that needs to be discussed. It seems reasonable to hope that a family that can negotiate a money policy among its members can go on to resolve other more complex issues later.

Inside and Outside the Family Business

As you decide to retire and hand over control of the family business, how do you fairly settle issues of ownership and decision-making powers among your grown children when some work for the company and some do not? Should those who work for the company be given a decision-making capacity, while those outside receive nonvoting shares?

Those outside the company may not know enough about the business to make reliable decisions and may be more interested in immediate cash payouts than reinvestment in the company's future. Clashes between family members with opposing interests seem likely. Can such confrontations be avoided by completely excluding from ownership those who do not work for the company?

These are hard choices to have to make on retirement. Children excluded from the family business may see you as putting the company's interests before theirs. Those who work for the company may resent your generosity toward those who do not. It's hard to find a rational pathway through an emotional minefield like this.

In many instances, family dynamics have been found to be more meaningful than the arrangements made by the retiring business owner. For instance, if sibling rivalries are strong, they are likely to continue, regardless of whether the individuals are included or excluded from the family company. Children who have perceived unfairness in your past treatment of them are likely to do so again.

You cannot make business decisions that factor in such complex emotional issues. This, of course, can happen in other situations also, such as in simply settling an estate.

You need to make decisions with the economic well being of your company in mind, and then explain these decisions to family members and recompense individuals who are being pushed aside.

One frequently successful way to accomplish this is for those included in the company to buy the stakes of those excluded from the company. You can structure the deal in terms that you see as fair. But you need to make sure that the outsiders fully understand that they are selling their ownership and not simply receiving a cash windfall.

For some families, the best arrangement is to give all children ownership and voting rights, regardless of whether they work for the company or not. Those outside should have the option of selling their shares in the company. Whether they can do so to non-family outsiders depends on how you set up the deal.

If you have total control and own all the shares of your family business, you can make all the rules. The better your children understand the business and the marketplace, the better they will understand the rules you lay down. The more they understand, the more likely they will be to perceive your efforts as fair to everyone while keeping the company economically healthy.

Be Prepared to Listen: Inheritor's Trusts

We have discussed how you can use trusts to pass on money to beneficiaries advantageously. In a new variation of this, beneficiaries are forming so-called "inheritor's trusts" in advance to receive inherited assets.

At the present time, your children or grandchildren may be wondering how best to approach you with this fresh concept. From their viewpoints, this could be an awkward conversation. They probably would not want you to think them too presumptuous about your intentions—unless of course you have already had a candid talk with them about your estate plan.

In addition, such a trust may be relatively expensive for them to set up, and they cannot fund it themselves for their own benefit. Your beneficiaries do not need to know what assets they will receive, but for an inheritor's trust to work, you have to make your bequest to the trust rather than to the beneficiary by name.

An inheritor's trust is really a form of dynasty trust. As we know, the assets of such a properly structured and funded trust can pass from generation to generation without additional estate taxes or generation-skipping taxes. This kind of trust also provides protection from creditors and divorcing spouses.

While the assets have to be substantial to make an inheritor's trust worthwhile, you don't have to be a Rockefeller. Like all dynasty trusts, however, inheritor's trusts may be subject to some future IRS tax laws or regulations.

Inheritor's trusts can be set up between parents and children, grandparents and grandchildren, and even between people without a family relationship. If you so choose, you can start funding an inheritor's trust during your lifetime.

Inheritor's trusts, like all other kinds, are very flexible. They are usually set up to give the beneficiary a lot of control and many options. The trustee is generally independent—an advisor, friend, or trust company—and has discretion over when and how the assets are distributed to the beneficiary.

The beneficiary may be made a co-trustee with power to make investment decisions and even to appoint a new independent co-trustee, although these powers need to be reviewed for tax consequences before being conferred.

Sound Advice

In reading this book, I hope you have discovered some new options or at least have come to look at some long-familiar things in a new way. By now, you've heard my warnings that regulations are at times intricate and that state laws often vary. In other words, you usually need professional advice.

If nothing else, a competent advisor can save you from expensive mistakes. Most experienced and knowledgeable advisors out-earn their fees by first and foremost pointing out pitfalls to be avoided. For many retiring people with meaningful assets, finding a good advisor could actually be considered the most important investment-related decision they can make.

AFTERWORD

Enhancing Life

It is one thing to discuss finances and planning in an abstract way, and quite another when you consider things that have happened in your own family or to people you know. In real life, the emotional impact of financial planning on familiar lives can stand out vividly.

I have a major ongoing experience like this in my family, but since the process still has not come to fruition, I will not describe it as though it has. Instead, I will use a story told to me by a friend.

When his father died, his will left everything to his mother, with the understanding that her will would divide everything fairly among their five grown children. The family loved her dearly, but did not have a high opinion of her investment and estate planning skills. They hoped that what their father had left her would last for her lifetime, and had little expectation of anything being left over for them.

Over the next few years, they were surprised at some of the questions she asked—mostly about business issues in the news and about what each of them really liked among the family possessions. They knew she had a financial advisor and she always turned down their offers of financial help.

When she died, 12 years after their father, they were amazed at the detailed way in which she distributed the family assets among her children. Even when they did not agree with her decisions, they could not contest them. Her wishes were clear and unambiguous.

The biggest surprise of all came a few days later, when her investments were evaluated at current market prices. She had left all five of her children financially secure.

When her husband died, she knew she needed help and was astute enough to find excellent professional guidance. Her family came to realize this, although one still believes she was secretly a financial genius. One could say, I suppose, that people who know they need advice and find it do have a certain kind of genius.

From her point of view, she was providing for her children's future and fulfilling her maternal role in an ongoing way. As for her grown children, her bequests have permitted some of them to take career and investment risks that they otherwise might not have felt free to take, the kinds of decisions (or risks) that have the potential to enhance their lives greatly.

In effect, her bequests have boosted these young people's bargaining power with life. They can afford to risk more and thereby have the possibility of greater return.

The benevolent effects of a bequest on a person's emotions and lifestyle can be more important than its actual dollar amount. Professional advisors like me see this every day. Similarly, we also see the huge emotional and lifestyle benefits of properly structured retirement investing and planning.

It immediately makes you feel great to know you have provided for the future. Your spouse may have had anxiety regarding this issue that you may not have been aware of. Now that worry can be eased.

Discuss your retirement investment and estate plans with your family. As grown children become familiar with financial realities in their own lives, they are likely to be increasingly concerned with your future well-being. Tell them they have nothing to worry about. Such knowledge lowers tensions and contributes to the enjoyment of family gatherings.

I would not go so far as calling this book *The Joy of Retirement Investing* (for all I know, a book with such a title may already exist!). But there is joy—as well as great satisfaction—in knowing that you have won the battle for survival and looked out for those close to you. This may fulfill some deep, early instinct in humans, because it is a powerful and abiding feeling. For many, it is the crowning achievement of their lives.

I think I can speak for all of my fellow attorneys and investment advisors when I say that having the opportunity to help our clients achieve goals that will last perhaps many generations gives us that same good feeling about what we do everyday.

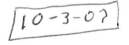

10-3-07

ABOUT THE AUTHOR

Jim Mosteller is the principal of Liberty Asset Management, a Registered Investment Advisory firm concentrating on wealth management and asset preservation. As founding partner of The Law Firm of Mosteller & Holmberg, P.C., he is a licensed attorney with a practice focusing on estate planning and elder law. Mr. Mosteller received his bachelor's degree in finance from The Ohio State University and his Juris Doctorate from The John Marshall Law School. He is a member of the Financial Planning Association, American Bar Association and National Academy of Elder Law Attorney's. Mr. Mosteller has presented investment and estate planning seminars to over 8,000 individuals and families and has personally worked with over 1,000 clients. He lives outside Chicago with his wife and three children.

To order additional copies of *If You Can't Beat 'em, Join 'em* or to contact the author about a speaking engagment, please call 800-569-0413.

NOTES

NOTES

NOTES